## Praise for *Chronic*

"An essential and nurturing guide for al and magickal practices with the realities of chronic pain or illness. Danielle Dionne, one of my favorite witches, shares her own journey and insights in a way that resonates deeply with those facing similar struggles. This book provides a compassionate framework that recognizes the physical and emotional terrains of chronic illness. Danielle offers spells and magickal practices for handling health with clear, actionable steps for readers to enhance their well-being and reclaim their personal power. *Chronically Magickal* is a source of hope and fortitude, a balm in the journey toward spiritual health and empowerment."

—**MAT AURYN**, author of *Psychic Witch* and *The Psychic Art of Tarot*

"This beautiful book came at the right time for me. I'm helping a family member navigate a new reality with a chronic illness. It's been challenging, but *Chronically Magickal* has become the perfect companion on this journey. The magickal rituals and potions have given us new tools to support both me and my loved one. I also appreciate the practical life advice and personal stories Danielle sprinkles throughout the book. Whether you struggle with health issues or caregiving, you'll want to keep this witchy book close at hand."

—**THERESA REED**, author of *The Cards You're Dealt*

"Danielle generously opens the door to her life, home, and heart to not only share her journey with you but offer the hard-earned wisdom that comes from truly living a magickal life and apply that magick to her health and well-being. If you are struggling with your health or with your magick in relation to your health, *Chronically Magickal* will be an immense support. Filled with great magickal wisdom and technique, the sections on the spirits of disease and the spirits of medication in particular will be powerful steps in the journey."

—**CHRISTOPHER PENCZAK**, bestselling author of the Temple of Witchcraft series

"A candid, raw, and (if you'll forgive me the pun) infectious perspective with actionable magical and mundane work that we can incorporate into not only our practice but our day-to-day lives, no matter how low on spoons we may be."
—**MORTELLUS,** author of *The Bones Fall in a Spiral*

"The practices, insights, and life experiences shared in *Chronically Magickal* are applicable to all of us.... This book offers an approach to claiming the fullness of being human that embraces the depths and the heights, the bright and the dark, and she offers practical methods to be as well as you can be. This is the first book I've read that truly applies the tools of witchcraft and magick to the long-term process of living well with the challenges of incarnation. Danielle's voice in the book is kind and gentle but is not sugar coated."
—**IVO DOMINGUEZ JR.**, author of the Witch's Sun Sign series

# CHRONICALLY MAGICKAL

## About the Author

Danielle Dionne is a professional psychic medium, witch, herbalist, and author of *Magickal Mediumship*. She is a High Priestess in the Temple of Witchcraft Tradition, serving as Scorpio Ministerial Deputy for death and dying, sacred sexuality, and ancestral connections. She trained under internationally renowned mediums, including John Holland and Tony Stockwell, and under prominent magickal and occult teachers such as Christopher Penczak and Devin Hunter. Additionally, she studied at the Arthur Findlay College, a spiritualist college in Stansted, England. She has been teaching psychic development since 2009. Danielle runs Seed and Sickle, an online space where she offers psychic and mediumship sessions, herbalism consultations, mentorship, and consultation on death care support and living with chronic illness. She lives in southern NH at Crossroads Farm, a spirited homestead that raises heritage breed livestock. She enjoys connecting with those like herself, who are magickal practitioners living with chronic illness. Visit her online at DanielleDionne.com and SeedandSickle.com.

# CHRONICALLY MAGICKAL

## NAVIGATING CHRONIC ILLNESS WITH WITCHCRAFT

DANIELLE DIONNE

WOODBURY, MINNESOTA

First Edition
First Printing, 2024

Cover design by Shannon McKuhen
Editing by Laura Kurtz
Interior sigil art by Danielle Dionne



**Library of Congress Cataloging-in-Publication Data (Pending)**
ISBN: 978-0-7387-6939-4



Llewellyn Publications
A Division of Llewellyn Worldwide Ltd.
2143 Wooddale Drive
Woodbury, MN 55125-2989
www.llewellyn.com

Printed in the United States of America

## Other Books by Danielle Dionne

*Magickal Mediumship: Partnering with the Ancestors for Healing and Spiritual Development*
(Llewellyn, 2020)

*Aquarius Witch: Unlock the Magick of Your Sun Sign*
(as contributor, Llewellyn, 2024)

*In memory of David Erwin. Rest easy, Magickal Uncle Dave.*

*And for all those who struggle but still persist.*

# Contents

# Exercises

# Acknowledgments

Thank you to Austin Dionne, my loving partner, and my family, for all the help they supplied so that I was able to write this book. I couldn't have done it without you.

Thank you to Chris Morris, for letting me pick your brain.

To my Temple of Witchcraft community, I'm so grateful for the camaraderie, support, wisdom, and love that you provide to me. You fill my cup.

To Heather Greene—thank you for your guidance and support digging into my drafts to get to the good stuff.

## Disclaimer

The material in this book is not intended as a substitute for trained, licensed medical or psychological advice. Readers are advised to consult their personal health care professionals regarding treatment, especially regarding the use of herbal medicine and plants. Avoid ingesting or working with plant material without the supervision of a trained medical professional if you are taking pharmaceuticals or supplements or are pregnant. For safer alternatives, please see the section on flower essences, which contain no medicinal components and are safe to use for everyone.

The publisher and the author assume no liability for any injuries caused to the reader that may result from the reader's use of the content contained herein. Common sense is recommended when contemplating the practices described in the work.

## You Are Not Alone

Chronic illness often goes hand in hand with mental illness. If you are struggling or don't have someone you can contact about your mental health, that doesn't mean you're alone. Remember that counselors are available 24-7 at the 988 Suicide and Crisis Lifeline in the United States. If you live in another country, visit www.findahelpline.com to find free, confidential support from a helpline, warmline, or hotline near you.

# Foreword

In a hotel in San Jose, I met a radiant being. Or two. It was PantheaCon in 2019, and all the authors you've ever heard of were crowded into a hotel to learn, laugh, shop, and connect. I had chatted into the wee hours (especially three time zones away from home) with Mat Auryn the night before, and he gushed about all the friends that he'd already seen on the first day.

"I have to introduce you to Danielle. You'd love her," he gushed.

And he was right. She walked in wearing a gauzy black ensemble covered in delicate flowers with a soft and reverent smile on her face, and I knew we'd get along famously. We talked most of the evening, and I felt like I'd made a friend for life. Someone who understood my struggles with chronic pain and chronic illness, someone who could listen without judgment, and someone with whom I could share my point of view about my struggles with both. You see, it can be hard to talk to someone who doesn't share those experiences. They mean well, but they can be unintentionally hurtful. They offer words they think are helpful ("Other people have it *so* much worse.") or can be unintentionally cruel ("Just wait until you're older!").

Danielle offered a kind ear, and you can hear that kindness expressed throughout this book. She is helping people all over the world through her discussions of chronic illness as a magical being. In the United States currently, 40 percent of people have at least one chronic illness. In magical communities, that number can seem low because we attract people who are not happy with the status quo and seek to change their life circumstances.

A book like this is so validating to find on the shelf because we feel seen and heard when someone else has had a similar experience. Hospitalizations, broken bones, wheelchairs, and the like aren't going to appear on a carefully curated social media post about the experience of Witches, Pagans, and other magical people. Danielle is coming from an authentic place that really resonates with magical practitioners of all kinds, because she not only has had experiences like these, but she's dealt with the onslaught of people who want to help by commenting on posts talking about a chronic condition. People in chronic illness spaces share experiences among each other, like having well-meaning friends and loved ones suggest getting better from everything from fad diets and yoga to "cleanses," therapy, and soul contracts. We have heard it all, I promise you. "My cousin's dog walker's best friend was cured by… [insert the current trend in health]." Danielle isn't suggesting "miracle cures" because if there were cures for these things, we wouldn't call them chronic illnesses. She offers a soothing tome of solutions that revitalizes and reinvents the idea of self-care for Witches.

Last year, I was lucky enough to run into her at TempleFest, a conference for the lovely people at Temple of Witchcraft, co-founded by Christopher Penczak, Steven Kenson, and Adam Sartwell. It was so empowering to have Danielle, who saw my cane and knew I was having a rough time with the weather that day, without me having to explain that many chronic conditions have a spectrum of mobility. She just knew and was able to make the accommodations I needed without arguing or explaining. After five years in a wheelchair and three years with platform crutches, sometimes I need my cane and sometimes I don't. It all depends on a variety of factors including amount and quality of sleep, immune system response, weather, recent amount of activity, planned amount of activity, and more. I never thought being disabled would require so much math in order to figure out how much energy I can expend in a given day.

Conference spaces should be handicap-accessible, not something we have to plan for. As followers of a nature religion, sometimes we experience the world out of doors. Being in touch with Danielle and having someone who genuinely understood what it meant to experience the conference with a physical disability was life-changing. Books like *Chronically*

*Magickal* give us the tools to see and experience the world in such a way that opens doors rather than looking in from the outside. Remember, being able-bodied is temporary: anyone can join our ranks at any time and almost always without warning.

To Danielle: You've accomplished a lovely book, and I'm so thankful for the work you have put into making witchcraft even more accessible—for me, for you, and for everyone who needs it. Blessings.

—Amy Blackthorn, author of *Blackthorn's Botanical Wellness: A Green Witch's Guide to Self-Care*

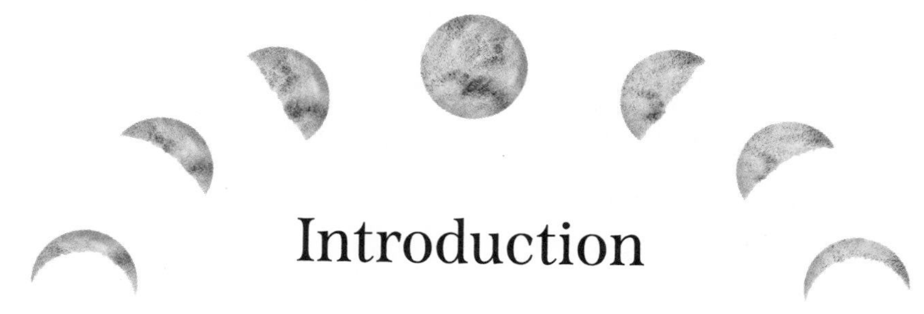

# Introduction

Having a chronic illness may feel like a solitary journey, but it's a lot more common than you might think. According to the American Hospital Association, an estimated "133 million Americans—nearly half the population—suffer from at least one chronic illness."[1] The CDC reports that six in ten adults in the United States have a chronic illness, while four in ten have two or more chronic illnesses.[2] Chronic diseases are defined broadly as conditions that last a year or more and require ongoing medical attention or limit activities of daily living or both. I knew there were others facing health challenges around me when I was in the throes of my initial blood disorder diagnosis, but I didn't know how to connect with or find others. I hope this book inspires witch folx to connect over shared experiences. Even though I don't know exactly what you have gone through, the fact that you've had to face difficult health news and the ups and downs that come with not feeling well is enough common ground for us to start somewhere. Promoting safe spaces to connect and share in person and online will provide some sense of connection in otherwise lonely and isolating times. I'm glad you are here. I'm glad you picked up this book for yourself or someone you know. I'm sorry for what you are going through. You are

1. "Health for Life," American Hospital Association, accessed February 22, 2024, https://www.aha.org/system/files/content/00-10/071204_H4L_FocusonWellness.pdf.
2. "Chronic diseases in America," Centers for Disease Control and Prevention, National Center for Chronic Disease Prevention and Health Promotion. Reviewed December 13, 2022, accessed February 11, 2023. https://www.cdc.gov/chronicdisease/resources/infographic/chronic-diseases.htm.

not alone in this. Let's make some magick together and find connection in our shared experiences.

## It Happened to Me

To share some background and context for what inspired this book, it would be helpful to know a bit about me and where I am coming from. At the time of writing this, I am in my late thirties and have been dealing with a rare blood disorder called thrombotic thrombocytopenic purpura (TTP) since 2021. Prior to that I've had autoimmune issues stemming back to being a teenager with no true diagnosis to date. Working diagnoses have been Still's disease, inflammatory arthritis, and suspected lupus or rheumatoid arthritis. Much like illnesses, I don't fit neatly in any one box. I have arthritis that affects me daily and flares that show up randomly and can be debilitating. I also have had migraines my whole life. I am someone who has and does wrestle with and confront depression, anxiety, trauma, PTSD, and eating disorders. After my TTP hospitalization in 2021, I was diagnosed with medical PTSD, and it has been a real beast to work on.

Knowing what you now know about me, let me share some of the things I'm proud to have accomplished: I've been a practicing psychic medium for more than fifteen years. I've been privileged to study with many international and famous mediums and spiritual teachers who have shaped and helped define my craft. A lot of my focus over the years has been on healing modalities for people and animals as well as death work. I have volunteered in hospice and oncology clinics and have had the honor of holding vigil for the dying on many occasions. I have led and cofacilitated Death Cafes and Mortal Musings discussion groups for many years. I have a background in research, data, and statistics, and I had a successful career working in health care culminating as the director of Quality, Infection Prevention, and Education at a community hospital.

I left the hospital to open a spiritual education center, Moth and Moon Studio, which I owned and operated for four years until the coronavirus pandemic in 2020. Throughout my tenure in health care, I worked evenings and weekends out of local metaphysical studios and shops teaching and providing readings and counsel for folks. It was wonderful to finally make that my full-time life.

My magickal studies have led me to several magickal traditions, but my main involvement and immediate community is with the Temple of Witchcraft. I am a high priestess in the Temple tradition, having graduated from their mystery school and seminary program. I serve as the ministerial deputy for the Scorpio Ministry, which is concerned with death and dying, ancestral connections, and sacred sexuality. I also am a member of the Sacred Fires tradition and work within and outside of a coven.

I am fortunate to live on a small homestead, Crossroads Farm, that raises heritage-breed livestock and maintains medicinal and magickal gardens. I am a practicing herbalist and homesteader. The caretaking of animals, land, and people is a dearly loved part of my life and work. My farm is home to cows, pigs, chickens, goats, bees, an elderly turkey, and a flock of Shetland sheep. I am a burgeoning shepherdess. I am also a licensed foster parent and in the process of adopting a toddler and teen. I identify as a bisexual and queer cisgendered woman married to a bisexual and queer cisgendered man. My pronouns are she/her.

## You're in Good Company

Let me emphasize this up front: This book will not heal you. I'm not offering promises that after reading and applying the methods, you will be healed. I still live with chronic illness. It's part of my daily life. However, there are things I've found to make my world better, and there are many things I'm continuing to work through now. I am not cured, I am not perfect, but I am a witch. Adam Sartwell, a friend and founder of the Temple of Witchcraft, is quoted to have said "Are you thinking like a witch?" When in my days of despair and pity parties (which are totally allowed and sometimes needed), this question has inspired me to zoom out and look at the bigger picture and what can be done about it. I hope that this book helps you to start thinking like a witch when it comes to the health challenges and daily dealings with your or someone you love's chronic illness. I also hope this book provides some direction and guidance to take matters into your own hands, especially in times where everything may feel out of control.

In my first book, *Magickal Mediumship*, I took my years of study and practice as a psychic medium and witch and distilled it into the book I wish I had read at the beginning of my spiritual journey or along my way to honing my practice. In this book I'm offering some vulnerability and sharing my personal and magickal experiences as a person living with chronic illness. I hemmed and hawed about if this is a book I wanted to write. I ultimately decided to do so because when I was in the throes of my autoimmune blood disorder ordeal, I looked to icons in my life who inspired me and went on to face chronic or difficult diagnoses. It made me feel less alone, and my hope is that I can offer that to you too.

## Trust the Process

I've accomplished a lot of things. And while I can appreciate credibility and its place in the world, a lot of what this book discusses will be informal compared to all the formal education and learning I've been lucky enough to have. A lot more of the content here has come from my own challenges and curiosities as well as what has motivated me or gotten me out of funks when I've been deep in them.

When I closed Moth and Moon Studio a few months into the coronavirus pandemic, I flung myself into farmwork and buckled down on homesteading. While it was a difficult time, in many ways it was one of the most profound years of my life as I got to work in tandem with the land, animals, seasons, and spirits by staying home and offering my services remotely. *Magickal Mediumship* came out at the end of 2020, and I had one of my most successful mediumship demonstrations alongside two of the best and well-respected mediums I know. I was living my best life in many ways. I even recall thinking, "Aha, I'm in my right alignment with self." I was physically strong and healthy, and I was kicking butt professionally. I was living at home, working the farm, cooking delicious food, having good sex, and doing all the best things. I was also about to enter the Temple of Witchcraft's fifth level and seminary program, which was an intensive year-and-several-months program.

At the beginning of the descent of the goddess work, the seven-week intensive that kicks off the yearlong solar work, I began to experience some weird health issues reminiscent of an autoimmune issue I had a decade earlier. I felt tired and began to have rashes and joint pain. As the program continued, I quickly began declining into what appeared to be an autoimmune flare-up. This was particularly upsetting as I had been milking my cow for a few months and was making grand plans for the coming spring and my farm. Soon I had to quit milking because my hands didn't work. I began to see my doctors and rheumatologists again, and while they clearly knew something was wrong, nothing definitive could be diagnosed. They thought perhaps it was lupus or rheumatoid arthritis, but these diagnoses can take a long time to be determined.

I continued to plow through my homework as best I could and felt like a terrible student. Have you ever done the minimum required, knowing you were capable of much more? That's how I felt again and again. I felt like I was a burden to my partner, who was having to take over farm chores on top of their full-time work. I felt helpless and hopeless in many ways. My spiritual practice became bare-boned, and while I knew the timing of this illness was particularly interesting with my Witchcraft 5 journey, I was not in great spirits.

Witchcraft 5 requires a lot of independent projects to complete, including a master spell, goal list, personal challenge from your teacher, and final project. I was stressed and worried that I was going to need to drop out, which would have been devastating. When I entered the program, I had been studying seven years in the school, and there would be a wait before I could get back in. I somehow managed through the first seven-week intensive. The thread and theme that emerged from the intensive work concerned healing maternal wounds in my bloodline and confronting motherhood. At this point I acknowledged the calling I had to be a mother in this lifetime, something I teetered on until this time. I wondered about having biological children and did some intense processing around this idea. I struggled personally with bringing life into a world with so much intensity and uncertainty. Physically, I wondered if it would even be possible. I thought about my genetics and potentially inherited mental and physical health concerns and the generational burden my biological descendants may be handed. I came to the conclusion at the last lesson before the solar work was to begin that biological children were not going to be a reality for me.

I was so sick of being sick. My symptoms started in February and come May, I was convinced it was time to move on from this "whatever." I managed to let my cows out to pasture on Beltane and officially announced I was on the mend and doing better on social media, not realizing how confused my brain actually was at the time. That same week I had a significant astrological transit in my chart that I interpreted as a blessing and boon. I have a Jupiter cazimi, where my natal Sun and Jupiter are on top of each other. It can be an incredibly lucky placement, so the day Jupiter was going to transit that position in my chart, I took it to be auspicious. It was, but not how I had hoped! I turned yellow on that Friday. (Well, Jupiter rules the liver, which I thought was interesting.) I had a doctor's appointment scheduled that Monday morning, so I decided to wait to see what was up.

Two days later, on Mother's Day of 2021, I was cooking dinner in my kitchen when I began to feel funny. Luckily, my partner, Austin, was home. My face went numb, and I looked at Austin and knew this was not good. I was having a transient ischemic attack (TIA) or what's known as a mini-stroke. We rushed to the hospital. After some testing it was determined that I had twelve platelets. I remember the nurse looking at that and saying it must be a mistake. I watched the team who was working me up for stroke symptoms realize this was something else happening. After a few consults and more tests, they told me they believed I had an extremely rare blood disorder and that I needed to go to Boston immediately—I was tanking. They started infusing blood, I was loaded in an ambulance, and I saw Austin standing in the parking lot as they closed the doors. That liminal ride became the end of my old life.

It's funny to think about now but wasn't at the time. I was sharing my death wishes with Austin as they were preparing me for the ride. Because this happened during COVID-19, he wasn't allowed to go with me. I have a death plan with information on body disposition and funeral ideas that my family knows about. However, it was unlikely that during the pandemic I'd have a home wake and natural burial, so I was trying to be nice by telling him it was okay if I was cremated and couldn't follow it with a service due to the state of the world. My brain automatically goes to death. My poor partner was in shock, and I was not helping the situation. I just didn't want him to feel the burden of it if I did die, and I very much could have. If I hadn't had the TIA ministroke, I would have been dead within twelve hours. People die of TTP because they can't figure out the problem, and it was an absolute miracle the small community hospital I went to figured it out and got me to where I needed to go in time.

I spent a month in the hospital where I received twenty-three plasmapheresis treatments, was placed on a biologic that targeted my wonky β-cells but also suppressed my immune system and increased my risk of infection, and was jacked up on loads of steroids. This was my baptism into a new way of living. I did not adjust well to it. However, one of the messages I received that deeply impacted how I look at the entirety of my health and situations as they unfold is this: my disease is TTP and, to me, it stands for "trust the process." And so that's what I do.

## It's Not Your Fault

As mentioned, this book is not meant to be a cure-all. I wish I could give that to you, but alas, not so. I can offer information on wise ways that can assist and promote healing, magickal efforts to help with all that comes from being ill, and self-empowerment techniques that can boost your energy, mood, and visions for your future. I believe my illness has provided learning opportunities to know myself better and guide me on my path, and I hope you may find that with yours. But there's something I would like to address before we proceed further. It's that good ol' belief that has swirled around people who get sick or have had bad things happen to them, the infamous "Is this my fault?" question.

*Did I do something bad to make this happen to me? Is this a lesson I must learn?* I certainly had these thoughts when sitting in my hospital bed pondering what the heck just happened to me. I sat with my thoughts and asked my spirits about it. I even asked spiritual friends to check on it for me because I was so distraught about it. *Did I anger the spirits? Had I deserved to almost die?* The truth that I believe—with even more certainty as I look around at the good company of folks who also have chronic illness—is that, no, it is *not* your fault. Seriously, if anyone tries to tell you otherwise, do not listen. It's cruel to say to someone with cancer that they deserve it and need to learn a lesson from it. Cancer can be a wonderful teacher, but you didn't *deserve* to get it, period. Do not internalize this. I almost did, and I see others who have struggled here too. It's not your fault.

## Who Is This Book For?

This book is for anyone who is currently or has struggled with being sick or is supporting someone going through illness. You might be someone with a chronic illness, invisible illness, chronic pain, autoimmune issues, ongoing mental health issue, terminal illness, or acute illness. While our experiences may differ, I hope I can provide something everyone can use in this book, whether your sick journey has been a long one or you are new to the party. If you are a magickal practitioner, excellent! I hope this book inspires you to try something new in your practice that can assist you with all that comes with illness. If you are new to magick and just starting out, hopefully these instructions will give you guidance and confidence to take some steps into manifesting change within your own world for the better.

If you are more experienced with your illness, you can skip over some of the sections of this book that look more familiar than for a newer person. On the other hand, it might be worth a once-over, as even someone like me, who has some years under her belt with being sick and such, can often use reminders.

# PART ONE
# CARING FOR YOU

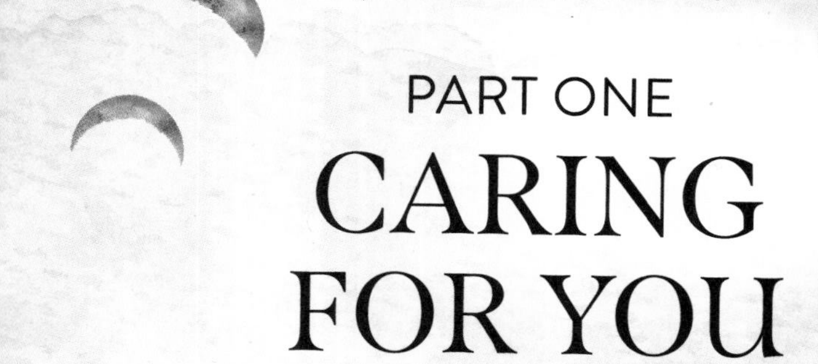

# CHAPTER 1
# Acquainting Yourself with Your New Reality

After a medical crisis or new diagnosis, you might feel a sense of detachment or even betrayal from your body. Your body is your lifelong partner, your closest companion. Finding out new information that something is not quite working as it should can be shocking to your system. Perhaps you've known something was off for a while without answers, and then suddenly you have one. You might know something is off now but don't have any answers, which can be equally frustrating. However your emotions toward your body show up for you, it's important to give your body the opportunity to share with you. I was desperately trying to convince myself that I was okay, that I was making up my illness and somehow all I had to do was try harder and I'd be fine. Maybe I was fine already. I was denying my body the chance to share its side of the story.

## Spoon Theory

If you're not brand new to chronic illness and fatigue, you're likely familiar with the spoon theory. The spoon theory is a way to illustrate the energy limitations that can result from living with a chronic illness. Using spoons as a unit of energy, the theory estimates how many spoons individual tasks require. It also helps people coping with chronic illnesses visualize their limited amount of energy per day. Writer Christine Miserandino came up with the idea explaining what it is like to have a chronic illness to a friend when she pulled out a bunch of spoons. The theory goes that each spoon represents a finite unit of energy.[3] Healthy people may have an unlimited supply of spoons, but people with chronic illnesses have to ration them just to get through the day. The spoon theory has become an easy way for chronically ill people to explain how they're feeling and coping day-to-day. It's a simple way to share with able-bodied people what a chronically ill person has capacity for in their life.

For example, when I wake up, I usually have an indicator of how my day is going to go. If I'm not feeling well, my joints and back hurt, or I have a migraine, I know it's going to be a low spoons day. I might have twelve spoons, ten, or, if it's really bad, five spoons. That's the amount of energy I have to spend. And on rough days, a task that usually might take one spoon now might take three, such as taking a shower. I would have to figure out the rationing of my spoons and what I am going to spend them on for the day. I recently had a terrible migraine day. I was hoping to write in my book, cook dinner, clean my living room and kitchen, and take the dogs for a walk. In the end, I only had enough spoons to take the dogs out to go to relieve themselves and go back to bed. My partner and family had to take over for me, as I just wasn't functional. Luckily, those days where it is so bad are rare, but frequently I'm running on an amount of spoons that doesn't cover my workload. Pacing is helpful here.

## Listening to Your Body

Listening to your body is an act of self-love. It takes a bit of patience and sometimes perseverance to get its essence, because it can be easy to disassociate with how the body feels when you feel constantly unwell. It's simpler not to tune in and ask what your body might require when you want to disown it.

An easy first step is to physically listen to your body. What is your body saying? Is it creaking or making noises? My joints often do this. If

3. Christine Miserandino, "The Spoon Theory," But You Don't Look Sick, accessed January 18, 2024, https://butyoudontlooksick.com/articles/written-by-christine/the-spoon-theory.

I'm looking to listen to them, I pause and see what comes to mind. Am I taking on too much or moving too much? Do I need rest? Recently my eye was twitching. I stopped and had a check-in with my body. Was this stress? Was I overly tired? Too much coffee? I finally realized I was stressed and my body was giving me the flag to do some deep breathing and listen to some calming chants to bring my amped-up self down a bit.

### EXERCISE
### Breathing into Blood, Body, and Bones

You may wish to record this exercise and play it back so you can experience it. You can alter what blood, body, and bones represent to you. This breath exercise expands my awareness and gives me a space to pause and listen to what it may be sharing.

**Step 1:** Listen and attune to your physical body.

**Step 2:** Take three deep, grounding breaths into your blood, body, and bones.

**Step 3:** Tune in to the blood that pumps through your veins, the life force energy. Notice how it feels flowing through your veins and arteries. See it as a snake slithering throughout.

**Step 4:** Tune in to your body, your flesh, your skin and muscles and tendons that you can touch and sense and connect you to you like a spider's web.

**Step 5:** Take a grounding breath into your bones, your structure, that which roots you like a strong tree.

## Taking Breaks and Avoiding Frying Yourself

Another area of readjustment when you have a chronic illness is figuring out how to reset. I used to be someone who could function with less sleep and keep chugging along. Now, I am not. One of my biggest struggles with chronic illness is not overdoing things. I used to be the queen of pushing myself to the limit and often with great success. I could pull all-nighters, work and play hard, and live my life to the absolute fullest. Now if I push too hard, I knock myself out of commission, sometimes for days. Pacing myself has become something I need to be much more cognizant of to conserve energy and be able to accomplish my days. I wish I had a super-helpful trick here about realizing your limits, but for me it's been a blend of self-care and body scanning I continue to do to check where my energy is at for the day.

### *Pacing*

If you are new to pacing, it is essentially the art of breaking down challenging things into more easily managed chunks. As chronic illness blogger Natasha Lipman defines it, "Doing the thing might be exhausting but doing little bits of 'the thing' until it's diminished is much easier."[4] Occupational therapists as well as physiotherapists are more understanding of this concept and often promote it, so you may have bumped into this idea before. Sometimes it might look like doing less to outside eyes and other medical professionals. It's truly not about doing less but breaking up the task so you can have more stamina. If you are someone like me, you might put your all into something and bang it out but at the cost of becoming a zombie for several days afterward. With pacing, taking your time and adding in things such as more frequent coffee or tea breaks allows you to get more done and not at your body's expense. Pacing also includes time for fidgeting. I'm a fidgeter, so allowing myself to do so enhances my concentration and the likelihood I'll finish something (she says while bouncing her restless leg).

Lisa Manary, my cofacilitator for the Temple of Witchcraft's Living a Magickal Life with Chronic Illness Discussion Group, shared some of her ideas on pacing with me:

> *Focus on your goals but never above your well-being. It's important to have goals in various areas of our lives. One thing I've learned from chronic illness is to take small steps as consistently as possible. And the most important thing I've learned from chronic illness is to*

4. Natasha Lipman, "Q&A: Pacing & Chronic Illness," Natasha Lipman, accessed on August 12, 2024, https://natashalipman.com/qa-pacing-chronic-lllness-resting-pain-fatigue/.

*continually ask myself, What is the next step I need to take right now? It may be as simple as sitting outside or as complicated as doing an entire ritual.*

## EXERCISE
## Dispelling Guilt

It is no fun feeling plagued with guilt about canceling plans at the last minute or not being able to accomplish something on time when you aren't feeling your best. I have noticed that I tend to overrationalize and share too much information and repeatedly apologize in these types of scenarios. But you don't owe anyone your life story or a big justification if plans need to change. I have been working in therapy on this for a long time and still need to remind myself to practice.

Here is a little charm I've crafted to keep myself in check when these feelings come up.

*I release the guilt of what is true for me,*
*And I no longer need to say "I'm sorry."*
*I am who I am, showing up as I can,*
*And when I cannot, I know I'm not less than.*

## Bless Your Pills

I went from being on zero medications to a lengthy list in a short amount of time. I had a lot of worries when it came to medications, and they had to do with some of the stigma I had seen around taking Western medicine from some of the herbalist communities I frequented. I felt like a failure because I couldn't naturally manage my health conditions. Wasn't that what herbalism was supposed to do? I was studying clinical herbalism and wanted to expand my practice when I started to get sick. I tried managing my symptoms with tinctures, teas, and supplements but still got worse.

I personalized my health challenges as a failure, but when I looked at folks I knew going through cancer treatments, I didn't see it as a failure for them. I had to recalibrate and look at the wholeness of my situation. It gave me a broader perspective on my new life and other people's lives as well.

Herbalism has its place for health and wellness, but so do pharmaceuticals. For goddess' sake, take your pills! If they help you and are making your quality of life and longevity improve, take them.

One way that I witch up taking my pills is to enchant my pillbox that I use for my weekly haul of medications. I encourage you to decorate your pillbox with sigils, signs, images, or anything that empowers this container for you. Mine has a promoting health sigil I created, a memory sigil to help me remember to take all my meds, and a sigil to reduce side effects. I also have a pretty and fancy pillbox that is much more attractive to me than the generic looking sterile ones often used in medical settings. There's nothing wrong with those boxes, but I didn't want to evoke that clinical feeling multiple times a day when I reached for the box.

Your pillbox can be a form of self-expression. Mine is a pretty sleek green (a color I associate with healing) with gold lettering. I purchased it online and have no regrets. I also think it's a better quality than the generic pillboxes, which I found break often or at least spill my pills by not closing effectively. I also anoint my pillbox with Power and Attraction Oil (found on page 80) to empower and bless it. You can craft your own with essential oils, herbs, and a carrier oil or even use flower essences. I dot the corners and middle in a five quincunx pattern.

## EXERCISE
## Pill Blessing

Another thing I like to do for my pills is bless them. Now that you have them stored in a container of power, every time you reload your medication, take a moment, hold the container of pills in your hands, and state your intentions out loud. Here is the blessing I use:

*In the name of the Goddess, God, and Spirit,*
*under the watchful eyes of the ancestors,*
*I ask for these pills to be blessed and consecrated in your good names.*
*May these pills aid in my overall health and well-being without side effects so I am able to function at my fullest capacity.*
*Help me remember to take my medications at the right times.*

*I am grateful for your assistance.*
*May there always be peace between us. So mote it be.*

## The Power of Thoughtforms

We should not underestimate the ability that our mindset has over our body. One of the biggest struggles I've witnessed when it comes to self-healing is the hold the mind can have over us—for good or bad. A close acquaintance whom I love and adore has several autoimmune diseases that frequently affect her, and she has flare-ups that come and go. She is also a magickal practitioner. When I've asked her what type of magick she does for herself regarding healing, she's told me she doesn't think to do so. When I look at this person's life, I see someone who has become their illness in many ways. If you were to meet this person, they would likely say, "Hi. I'm so-and-so, and I have these diseases"—if not out loud, the energy definitely emanates from them. It is her reason for not going out, for not pursuing her passions, for staying complacent. Her mind is firm that she is not getting better and that even the better days are not good. She struggles with depression and executive function challenges but doesn't get help. Ironically, she thinks of the spirits of disease as monsters, like the illustrations covered in the spirit section. I wonder about that effect on her relationship to disease.

I mention this case as an example where getting the mind in order can greatly benefit the body. I don't believe you can think positively into getting rid of a longterm diagnosis, but I do think working on mental health, working on self-limiting beliefs, and taking back some control starts with your thoughts, and that can influence how you feel.

What about magick? Does doing magick help heal? Yes, I believe it can. I believe miracles happen, and their sources vary. Working with magick and illness can be so much more than just curative. It presents an opportunity to focus on quality of life, finding the right health care team for you to thrive with, and finding the right jobs to support you financially while accommodating your needs. It's about finding friends and a community to feel a connection with who accepts you as you are. It's about finding ways to make life easier on you. Most of all, magick is there to empower you and catalyze change.

## Daily Life Changes

Being sick can wreak havoc on activities of daily living. Suddenly your life looks different and you need to figure out new ways to manage. In this section we'll walk through some of those areas and pose some mundane and magickal solutions to help you adjust to the new normal.

### *Food*

When dealing with chronic illness, food can be challenging. When it feels like aspects of your life are out of control, figuring out food is rough. It can also be an opportunity to gain some control. I love cooking, but there are times when I do not have the reserves to cook a full meal from scratch. Finding ways to hack meal creation for not just myself but my family is an ongoing quest I find myself on as I confront my new normal. Some things I have found helpful include modifying food prep. There are times when standing and chopping vegetables is not an option.

To work through the process, I've tried to meal plan and back my process up. I might chop one or two things in the morning and then after some time or a break, come back to finish. Grocery stores often sell chopped veggies to use in cooking. While they may cost more, they are potentially a good option for you to skip this step. And though I love to use fresh ingredients when I can, sometimes you can save money and effort by going with the frozen version and using those ingredients in your meals. Using frozen foods also solves the challenge of getting fresh food if you are not feeling well enough to go to the store.

Another incredibly helpful grocery store hack that came out of the pandemic was grocery delivery and to-go services. I use my local grocery store's to-go option for most of my shopping. It costs less than five dollars to have someone pick out my groceries, and I just drive to pick it up and have them load it into my car. It's amazing and was an incredible blessing when I just didn't have it in me to physically enter the store. If you want to skip the pickup, you can also now get groceries delivered to you. This does cost more, but it may be worth it to get through what you're going through.

Other things I try to do to keep my food fresher for longer so things don't go bad as quickly is to put bread in the freezer. I can take out what I plan to use when I need and put it in the toaster. I do this with pita bread when I want hummus. I also keep some easy food options stocked so if I'm having a harder day, I can deviate from my meal plans and still be able to feed myself and my family. Even if the meals aren't as healthy, they might on that day be healthier for me. Chronic illness is about finding balance and what works, and this is an area that certainly highlights this truth.

Like most of my family, I'm neurodivergent, and sometimes it causes its own extra challenges. There may be only certain foods one person is willing to eat, and planning around that can put extra constraints on meals. I make a meal plan each week, and even though I think it's a pain in the butt, it really helps my neurodivergent brain process what the plan is each day, and I can work through constraints and conveniences. I have a hard time making on-the-fly decisions, but if I plan ahead, choose things that meet the requirements of my family, grocery shop online, and pick it up, I tend to have good results. I don't forget to buy the things I need from the grocery store because I got distracted or buy a bunch of extra stuff I don't need. Having a plan also lets me choose coupons and shop the flyer deals so I end up saving more than I would if I just went to the store. This may seem mundane, but it frees up so much time and energy that energetically makes my home and self feel better.

### *Clothing Yourself*

Wearing clothes that feel good affects your energy and how you feel and view yourself. When you are well, you might have a signature style and even special ritual attire. When you become sick and don't have energy to put into wearing these types of clothes, new solutions must be explored. Surely, everyone is wearing some clothes at home or in the hospital, but how many feel good about their outfits while they are sick? This was something I recognized when things got difficult, and now I'm better equipped. I used to have only a few pairs of pj's. Some were cute and some were sexy, but they were not the type of clothing you would want to wear if you were sick. If you are often sick, you need sick clothes.

I now have as many comfortable sick clothes as I do regular, ritual, and dress-up clothes, which was a huge shift for me. When I was homebound, I didn't feel up for dressing up but didn't want to be in just pajamas either. This is when things like loungewear can help. Finding comfy pants that I wasn't afraid to wear in public if I had to became a quest. I was never one to really wear t-shirts unless I was out in the barn, but I needed to expand that part of my wardrobe. I began opting for graphic tees with witchy designs and band T-shirts I liked. They were not my true style, but they were passing. They connected me to parts of me that were still me, which helped me accept how things were. And what was nice was that I could sleep in them and wear them during the day without feeling like I looked like I slept in them. Try to have a supply of clean clothes to wear. Find ways to save your spoons but also maintain good hygiene. I'll go over some of my tricks for laundry when discussing managing mess. The main takeaway here is to get your sick outfits in order and rock those bad boys around the house.

### *Comfort Objects*

Comfort objects can be helpful at making you feel better when you are ill or during transitions. They could be a stuffed animal or a comfortable blanket. Children often have comfort objects, and adults can have them too. A few years back, I was in the throes of getting in touch with my inner child, which was surprisingly a challenge. I have never been one for keeping toys or stuffed animals, but perhaps that has to do with the amount of growing up I had to do at a young age.

When I was in the hospital, my friend Mat Auryn sent me what was essentially a room full of stuffed animals for all my farm animals I needed to be away from while I was sick. It was incredibly kind, and at first I felt silly with all the doctors and hospital staff commenting on the pile of stuffed animals I had rapidly acquired. But you know what? I really liked them! I even slept with the opossum on my bed. It helped the little kid inside me who was scared and afraid of what might happen. It's funny how adults can rationalize a situation to make it practical and logical. On the inside I was still afraid of all the chaos that was happening. In truth, I didn't have control like I could pretend I did. At night when I was alone and couldn't sleep in the hospital, I found holding my comfort opossum helped me feel much better. I slept better too!

I recommend giving comfort objects a try. If you can't wrap your brain around hugging a stuffed animal (I recommend that too), try a comfy blanket that has a nice feel and pleasing color. Weighted stuffed animals and blankets can also be soothing. You might get in the habit of making yourself a cup of tea, making a simmer pot so the house smells good, burning a scented candle, or having some of your favorite snacks around for when you want to feel comforted.

### *Rest*

Pacing or taking time to rest don't have to look a particular way. Rest can be switching from the activity you've set out to do. For example, rest from writing this book can look like stretching and then checking on my cows. Or it could be taking a quick moment to cleanse myself with sacred smoke. It doesn't always have to be silent and still or laying down in a dark room. I often find breaks of rest to be moments outside, getting some fresh air. Sometimes it's putting my head down for ten minutes. Taking breaks how you see fit when you are pacing yourself or just need to switch things up can have significant beneficial results. You can also add in moments of ritual or magick to these restful moments. Light a candle, take some deep cleansing breaths, or align your cauldrons (see page 40). If you are not someone who normally tries these things, give it a shot. I was surprised at how well it has worked for me. It sounds easy and simple, and it is. With payoff!

### *Sleep*

Let's face it: sleep is important. Some of us with chronic illness love to sleep and could sleep all day. For others, sleep is elusive. Though we try, we don't ever quite seem to get the restful sleep we desperately need. Doing your best to have a routine bedtime can benefit your body, because it will begin to expect that you will lie down for bed at a certain time and eventually fall asleep. If you are having trouble sleeping, sometimes sleep aids can help. Use headphones and listen to sounds like binaural beats or white or green noise to help you relax into sleep. Aromatherapy has also been very helpful. I use lavender essential oils, sprays, and lotions to help calm me and prepare me for sleep. There are also teas with lavender in them that taste delicious and have a calming effect. I hang mugwort over my bed to help support my dreams. Find what works for you!

If you are sleeping a lot, it may be just what your body needs. It can also be side effects from medicines or part of your illness, so it's always good to run it by your doctors. Sometimes you may have chronic illness with depression. If that's the case, having a mental health professional evaluate you is also a helpful idea because sleeping more than usual can be an indicator.

## EXERCISE
### Comfort Object Talisman

Talismans are charms used to bring in energy or manifest something. You can add some magick to your mundane comfort items by creating a comfort object talisman. I used a weighted stuffed animal, but use what works best for you.

#### You will need

A comfort object such as a stuffed animal, blanket, or special mug
Smoke to cleanse the comfort object; this could be incense, palo santo, or other sacred herbs
Power and Attraction Oil (recipe on page 80)

**Step 1:** Light your media to create sacred smoke. Take your comfort object and pass it through the smoke three times, saying aloud,

*I cleanse and clear this comfort object.*
*May it be clear for me to program. So mote it be.*

**Step 2:** Hold the comfort object in your hands. Speak aloud your intentions for the object. You could say,

*I ask in the name of the Goddess, God, and Great Spirit, under the watchful eyes of the ancestors, that this object be consecrated to manifest comfort, healing, and peace within and around me. I ask that this energy promote helpful, harmonious energy for my highest healing good. Thank you to all those who aid in this work. So mote it be!*

**Step 3:** Use your comfort object to manifest your goals.

## Sex and Chronic Illness

The topic of sexuality when living with chronic illness isn't discussed enough. Being diagnosed with a chronic illness can be devastating and affect every aspect of life, including sexuality. Becoming ill may cause you to feel less confident or attractive due to the changes in your body from illness or medication. Worrying about how your partner now feels about you can lead to anxiety and stress. You may have less energy or a reduced sex drive. There may also be worries about pain or your own comfort level with your body.

I'm here to say that it truly sucks when some or all these things are true. However, I try to remember that things do not stay the same forever. If you are going through a rough patch, that is okay. Try talking to your partner about your feelings. I know this is a vulnerable and often taboo topic, but it is your life. It took me a long time after my initial hospitalization to even begin to think about having sex again. And then once I did, I wasn't particularly feeling good about my body. I was also worried my partner would no longer look at me the same way after having to take care of me.

What worked well was having honest conversations about how I was feeling and how my partner felt about it. It helped take away some of the pressure I was putting on myself to try being "normal." The truth is, this *is* my new normal, and there are going to be ups and downs. That doesn't mean it is the end of intimacy. You will need to figure out how this works for you.

I also recommend talking with your doctor about how you are feeling. I was able to make some medication tweaks that helped me feel better. In addition to doctors, find a counselor or trained therapist to help you process what has happened and explore this topic with the help of an outsider.

Expressing your feelings for your partner through acts of kindness is another way to feel close to them that can foster connection.

## EXERCISE
### Love Yourself Attraction Bath Soak

One way to boost feeling better about yourself that can even be used as an aphrodisiac is the Love Yourself Attraction Bath Soak. Use this soak when you wish to feel better in your body, mind, and spirit or in preparation for intimacy, which can include sexual activities as well as cuddling and connecting in nonsexual ways.

#### You will need

Mason jar or container
Mixing bowl
Spoon for mixing
½ cup dried rose petals
½ cup dried calendula
½ cup dried lavender
½ cup coarsely ground sea salt
½ cup Epsom salt
¼ cup baking soda
¼ cup neutral oil (sweet almond, jojoba, olive, or sesame)
4 drops of lavender essential oil
5 drops of Power and Attraction Oil (recipe on page 80)

**Step 1:** Blend the dry ingredients in a mixing bowl. As you add each ingredient, state aloud its name, and thank it for aiding in this bath.

> *Rose, thank you for adding your beauty and power to this bath.*
> *Blessed be.*
> *Calendula, thank you for adding your bright spirit to this bath.*
> *Blessed be.*
> *Lavender, thank you for adding your calming presence to this bath.*
> *Blessed be.*

*Sea salt, thank you for adding your cleansing properties to this bath. Blessed be.*

**Step 2:** Slowly pour in the oil of your choice as well as the essential oils and Power and Attraction Oil. Stir to combine. Say aloud,

*Power and Attraction Oil, thank you for amplifying the energies mixed here and for boosting my power and attraction through this bath. Blessed be.*

**Step 3:** Hold your hands over the bowl of combined ingredients and say aloud,

*I consecrate and bless this bath so I may feel more myself.*
*Let the power within me be revealed,*
*Let the love within me come forth,*
*Let me feel my own beauty, radiance, and power. So mote it be!*

**Step 4:** Add the mixture to the containers. Label them with their ingredients and the date.

**Step 5:** Add a couple of tablespoons to a drawn bath and enjoy.

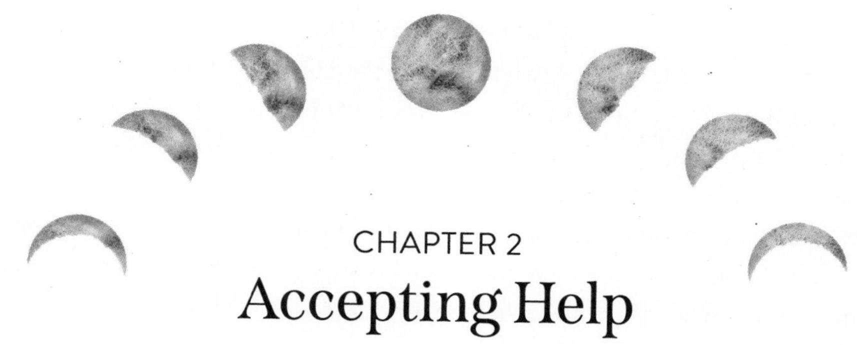

CHAPTER 2

# Accepting Help

One of the hardest lessons I had to work through in my "new life" as someone chronically ill was how to allow others to help me. I am naturally a helper. If you need support, I'm there for you. Do you need help with your home and clutter? I'm your girl. Last minute change of ritual plans and you need someone to wing a main role? Sure thing! I am happy to chat or provide suggestions if I'm knowledgeable in the subject. But being on the asking end is tough stuff.

When I was in the hospital, people asked how they could help, and it was incredibly taxing on me to figure out what they could do. I like to have control but don't like people in my house, so I was having to relinquish a lot out of the gate. We had two small puppies who came to live with us right before I tanked health-wise, and they required a lot of care in addition to the needs of our entire farm. I thanked people but declined a lot of help and later deeply regretted it. I was too proud and embarrassed to take folks up on their offers. I had two magickal Kitchen Witch friends who brought my partner and I food, and it was so helpful. It meant so much to me and what was nice is that they didn't pressure me, they just came by and dropped things off. The food was so delicious, and you could feel the love.

## The Art of Asking

One of my favorite musical artists and general badass humans is Amanda Palmer. I've always been impressed with her unabashed ability to be her genuine, raw self. She is adored and hated for this attribute. She wrote a book that I honestly struggled with while reading, *The Art of Asking.* I reread this book after my hospitalization and took some strength away from its boldness. One of the quotes that deeply struck me from her work sums up the discomfort and trouble with asking for things. It resonated at my core with the fears I had asking for help:

> *Everybody struggles with asking. From what I've seen, it isn't so much the act of asking that paralyzes us, it's what lies beneath. The fear of being vulnerable, the fear of rejection, the fear of looking needy or weak, the fear of being seen as a burdensome member of the community instead of a productive one.*[5]

Grapple with those apples! Whether we like it or not, we need to become comfortable with the uncomfortable. And those underlying fears need to be confronted. Sometimes the crisis pushes us to do just that.

### EXERCISE
### Asking for Help

If you find the idea of asking for help when you need it to be intimidating, try this exercise to move through the vulnerability.

#### You will need

Pen and piece of paper
Cauldron or fireproof container
Lighter or matches

**Step 1:** On the piece of paper, write down all the reasons, fears, worries, shame, guilt, or anger that comes up about asking for help or assistance. Do not stop writing until you are thoroughly finished. Get it all out.

5. Amanda Palmer, *The Art of Asking: How I Learned to Stop Worrying and Let People Help* (New York: Grand Central Publishing, 2014), 13.

**Step 2:** Place the paper in the cauldron or fireproof container. Do this exercise outside or somewhere safe indoors where your fire alarm will not be affected.

**Step 3:** Say aloud,

> *In the name of the Goddess, God, and Great Spirit, I ask that these reservations be taken from me. Help me, help myself. May I learn to ask without fear, like I am asking you now, for the assistance I require. May all fear, shame, guilt, anger, and worry be removed. I am grateful for your aid. May there always be peace between us. So mote it be.*

**Step 4:** Light the piece of paper on fire. Watch it burn down to ashes.

**Step 5:** Dispose of the ashes into the wind or soil.

## Organizing Help in Crisis and Times of Need

One idea to organize help in the instance of hospitalization or a health crisis is a meal train. Don't be like me and decline when others offer to organize for you. You can create your own or use the websites such as Mealtrain.com to set up a schedule to arrange meal coverage. Friends, family, and community can take assigned spots to cook or cover a meal. When you are sick or in crisis, not worrying about cooking or paying for expensive takeout is a blessing.

Another way to support someone in crisis or going through a rough patch is to take on their time-consuming tasks. I live on a farm and when I was sick, all the nonessential farmwork was tabled, including mowing the lawn and trimming the bushes. My partner was taking care of me and driving to Boston every day, so they were also unable to work on these things. A leader in my witchcraft community arranged to have our lawn taken care of, and it was an incredibly kind gesture that really addressed what we needed. If he hadn't asked, he would never have known how much of a stressor it was to us at the time.

## Finding Support

Once you have let the reality of being sick set in, it's a whole process to understand your navigation settings. Support systems are one of the most important resources you can have, especially out of the gate. Being sick takes a toll mentally, but emotional support can often be overlooked because the focus is on physical fixes. I highly encourage seeking emotional support, especially during difficult times. Having trusted and knowledgeable medical providers is also imperative. Trusting that you're in good medical hands can make all the difference when faced with acute and chronic medical needs. And beyond your emotional needs and medical needs, it's beneficial to find ways in which you can be supported magickally through your illness. It's important to address multiple types of needed support in your life, mundane and magickal.

### *Emotional Support: Peer Groups*

Find people who have similar health issues as you. I found TTP and lupus support groups online and on Facebook. In truth, these support groups have been mostly helpful but when I was first diagnosed, they made me scared. There were lots of people sharing stories of loved ones who had died from TTP and those currently going through episodes where they were fearful and helpless. It wasn't the best news for someone hopped up on lots of steroids just trying to see what life was like outside of TTP episodes for others like her!

My advice is to take things with a grain of salt. Some people look on the bright side of life and view the world with rose-colored glasses. Others, and many I saw in these groups, were speaking from a defeated and depressed state. Chronic illness can walk hand in hand with depression and anxiety, and I certainly can attest to it. Keep it in mind while reading all the comments, and look at the overall pool of folks. I found that most people with my disease were living their lives. Modified, yes, but out there with their families and friends, working in careers they loved, and achieving their dreams. I realized my diagnosis wasn't a death sentence and that I had good and bad days to look forward to but nothing is static.

Cycles and seasons are often observed with folks with chronic illness. For me, it was about learning to honor the cycles which were hard and difficult but then knowing my personal spring would come again and I would eventually feel better. Seeing others in the support groups share their highs and lows was ultimately helpful and gave me some ideas of how not to handle myself. I didn't want to overidentify with my disease. I didn't want to wear a badge proclaiming "this is me" like some other so-called TTP warriors I saw posting in the group. I wanted to not think about or name my illness. I wanted to shrink it. I believed the less I thought about it and the less energy I spent with it, it would somehow diminish its power over me. I also think this might have been my denial phase, but it was a conscious choice I made at the time.

You may feel completely opposite, and that is okay! You may want to shout from the rooftops, claiming your illness and owning the reality of your life. Both viewpoints can be helpful, and ultimately finding the right balance will be the best outcome possible.

Support groups can be great places to connect with others with a similar diagnosis or health challenges. Specialist offices will sometimes have planned groups you can attend in office or online. Sometimes you can find them online with folks from all over.

### *Emotional Support: Therapists*

While support groups can be helpful and you may meet people there you can talk to or rely on for emotional needs, I also suggest making a solid plan for your mental health and emotional support needs. For your mental health, it could be a short bout where you need to work through something with the help of another or longer-term therapy sessions where you have a steady person there to listen and work with you as you continue your health journey.

### *Emotional Support: Friends and Family*

Identifying your friend circle whom you want to trust and keep close while you are going through a health crisis and for longer-term support is sometimes a challenging but necessary process. When I was first diagnosed with TTP and was hospitalized, I created a group chat about how I was doing. I figured my close friends would be there for me and wanted to share what was happening. One of the hardest parts of becoming a person with chronic illness was realizing that not everyone is comfortable being friends with you when it gets hard. One of my best friends whom I deeply cared about at the time went silent. They stopped replying to my messages, and it hurt me so much. I rationalized that they were uncomfortable with illness and death and generally not someone who could get into the trenches with others when it was messy. I still care about this person, and to this day we've only exchanged a few hellos, and I have yet to see them in person. These instances are disappointing and an example of another small grief that must be mourned.

One important note about family and friends: it is important to set boundaries. Protecting myself from oversharing was something else I faced when going through my health debacle. Just as some friends back away when the going gets tough, sometimes other folks step up. I had some wonderful experiences befriending folks I didn't know that well after coming home from the hospital. At the same time, someone I didn't want to let into my circle was vying for information about how I was doing. It prompted conversations about what permissions I gave for people to share information about my health. Eventually, the person trying to get info about my hospitalization through my partner got the hint when he stopped responding. It can sometimes be hard to limit what gets shared and with who. I asked to be in control of sharing, and one way was to put out statements from time to time on social media that could be shared with anyone. This kept people from bombarding me and hopefully quelled some of the prying.

### *Medical Support: Doctors*

Finding the right medical providers and even medical supplies can be an ongoing challenge for people living with chronic illness. While finding a mental health professional can be daunting and you might need to get to know a few before finding the right one, it's harder with doctors and even more so specialists. I recommend finding a primary care provider (PCP) who gets you. This doctor is on your side and will be there with you through the potentially numerous episodes you may face from your chronic illness. If you don't respect them or they don't respect you, fire them. Break up with them. However you see the relationship, find a provider who has your back and your best interests at heart. I find I can put up with more challenging specialists knowing my PCP will listen to me. That being said, if your specialists are rude or uncaring toward you, you can seek out someone different. The problem with searching can be access. I ended up receiving my treatments in Boston, about an hour away from my local hospital systems. I was lucky to have access to world-class health care and multiple hematologists and Harvard researchers at my side during my crisis. It may be more challenging to get a second specialist opinion depending on where you live. Do your best to get yourself a team that listens to you and is knowledgeable about your condition.

As with friends and family, you need to set boundaries with medical professionals. I had a challenging experience with a hematologist who took great interest in me because my case was "extremely rare." When he left the practice, he wanted to keep me on a special list of patients he would continue to see, as I was a "collectible" to him. I remember being flattered and horrified by this. While I respected his knowledge, his rapport, and ability to listen to me, I knew something was wrong with the idea of putting me in grave danger if I had an allergic reaction to my medicine.

For a while, I was without a specific doctor, which gave me the opportunity to use witchcraft to draw in the best possible fit. I knew I wanted a female doctor who was knowledgeable, kind, had good rapport with patients, and would stick up for me if needed against the slew of other doctors and residents who would ultimately take care of me if I was ever hospitalized again. And she appeared! After that, I was happy moving on to my new provider, who is much more engaged with me and is a great listener. Don't settle—you deserve better. Some physicians have some catching up to do when it comes to patient satisfaction, which they are assessed on regularly. Don't be afraid to take those surveys. Be honest with them, as it can only help things improve.

### *Magickal Support: Witches and Healers*

If you are in a magickal community, you may be included in a healing altar or healing list for folks to send out healing energy to you if it's been shared that you are in need. This is usually done in good faith by community leaders or individuals who wish to help out. It's a kind and often well-appreciated gesture. However, I again encourage you to exercise your bodily autonomy and reflect on whether this is something you would like to be included in. It's okay to be okay with it at some points and not at other times. Most people sending energy will ask for it to be received for the highest healing good or to be accepted only if that is the individual's highest will. I like including this if I am sending healing to someone.

The reason I encourage your consent is because consent is always important. When I was in the hospital, I was grateful for the healing sent my way and gave permission for it to be sent. Later, when I was going through some of the grief and denial stages of being diagnosed, I didn't want my name included on the healing lists and sort of went silent for a few months. I didn't want people to see my name on the list and pity me or think I wasn't doing well. Even though I wasn't doing well, I didn't want that to be how the community thought of me. It's okay to feel how you feel and your wishes should be respected. Later, I added my name back on the list and once again appreciated the energies being sent my way.

### *Magickal: Divination and Outside Help*

If you feel there might be something energetically off with you or you need some guidance, I recommend asking a trusted divination system to help you determine appropriate actions to remedy your situation. If you are having trouble discerning for yourself what needs to happen or your divination is unclear, consider seeking someone you trust who is trained in energy work, healing, or magick to help you. There is no shame in seeking outside assistance. Often, it is best to have someone help you see clearly if you are off energetically. They may be able to do a healing or cleansing for you or guide you to the best actions.

## Growing around Grief

Grief models are worth exploring a bit—like it or not, grief comes with the territory of having a chronic illness. Most people think of Swiss psychiatrist Kübler-Ross's five-stage grief model that was based on her work with terminally ill patients and included in her book, *On Death and Dying.* The five stages include denial, anger, bargaining, depression, and acceptance.[6] This model has been updated to reflect that these stages are not linear, and not everyone goes through all stages. It's okay if you do, though, as I did with my blood disorder diagnosis. Mine were mostly in that order as well, though I bounded around from anger to depression a fair bit. And I definitely hit the bargaining stage hard when I'd tell myself, "I'm going to be the exception. I'll never be hospitalized again." Wrong. It's just rough getting to acceptance and staying there.

Another grief model that I think explains chronic illness well is the "growing around grief" model created by grief counselor Lois Tonkin. Tonkin came up with the model after speaking to a client about the death of their child. The woman told Tonkin that, at first, grief filled every part of her life. She drew a picture with a circle to represent her life and shaded it to indicate her grief. It was all-consuming. She had thought that as time went on the grief would shrink and become a much smaller part of her life. But what happened was different: the grief stayed just as big, but her life grew around it. There were times when she felt the grief as intensely as when her child first died. But there were other times when she felt she lived her life in the space outside the circle.[7] This fits with my experience of having an all-consuming illness that takes up your whole mind and existence with its presence. After some time, you begin to understand it and grow around it. It doesn't go away, but you become better equipped to deal with it and take on new challenges or pick up your old ways. The size of your illness stays the same, but *you* grow.

6. Elisabeth Kübler-Ross, *On Death and Dying: What the Dying Have to Teach Doctors, Nurses, Clergy and Their Own Families* (New York: The Macmillan Company, 1969), 265.

7. Lois Tonkin, "Growing around Grief," Cruse Bereavement Support, accessed July 29, 2023, https://www.cruse.org.uk/understanding-grief/effects-of-grief/growing-around-grief.

## Mourning Little Deaths

When you are diagnosed with a chronic illness, it can bring up so much once you have a moment alone to reflect. The first time it started to sink in for me, I was in my hospital room three days after getting there and finally being able to think a bit more clearly. I was alone and unable to have visitors, as it was during the coronavirus pandemic. I realized that things would never be the same again for me. This was the first little death.

There would be so many more little deaths. I mourned the life I might have lived and for how things could have been in the future. It doesn't mean I don't have a future, but it's likely the future will always hold arthritic hands and knees, fatigue, regular blood testing, and lots of medications. It's okay to feel sad for yourself. We live in a culture that doesn't do death or grief particularly well. For a while, I tried to ignore my feelings about my illness. In fact, I tried not to say or name my illness as much as possible. I didn't want to claim this illness as my own. And while that worked for some time, ultimately I do own these illnesses. It has gotten better when I've tried to partner with my illnesses rather than ignore them. They have lessons to teach me, and I do better acknowledging them. For example, when I am experiencing chronic fatigue, it teaches me to go slow and focus on what truly matters and deserves attention from me. I can't spare extra energy, so it must go to the essential needs. It challenges me to put my life in perspective.

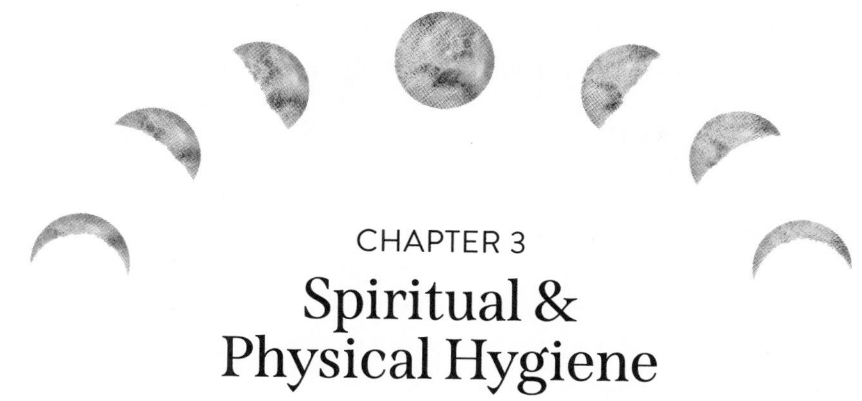

CHAPTER 3

# Spiritual & Physical Hygiene

Hygiene in general is an important task that can sometimes take a lot of effort for those with chronic illness. Spiritual hygiene can feel the same way. Cleansing and purification is an important part of doing the work, as it can promote health and also remove, refresh, and reset energies. I know I frequently need to do this just to feel some relief, which is why it should not be overlooked or taken for granted. Setting up protection magick for yourself and using wards can also be useful to chronically magickal folx. These techniques are primarily used to block out unwanted energies and influences. In this section we'll explore some ideas for both cleansing and protection that can help you energetically manage yourself for the better.

## Spiritual Hygiene

One simple and frequently used technique is a quick overall assessment and check-in with my body's energy through a body scan. I discussed the body scan in my previous books and how helpful it is when you begin doing a mediumship session because it gives you a baseline for how you are feeling.

Sometimes I disassociate from my body without meaning to. I might not be listening to all of my parts and what they are trying to communicate to me. Doing a slow, progressive relaxation technique with a body scan to notice how each area of my body feels and is showing up for me gives me some useful information. If I'm trying to see how I am feeling in my body, I start at the top of my head and slowly move down. Some areas I sense might be warm or cool feeling, or I might sense tiredness and achiness. Noticing which areas are standing out gives me a chance to check and listen for any needs. Maybe I'm dehydrated and have the start of a headache coming on. That prompts me to drink some water. Maybe I'm hungry. Maybe I need to give my bad knee a rest because my arthritis is acting up. Scanning provides intel for when we become desensitized to our needs because we regularly do not feel well.

A body scan is also useful as a self-diagnostic energetic assessment and can be expanded to include your emotional, mental, and energetic states. If you find areas of your body that need addressing on physical, emotional, mental, or spiritual levels, it's best to place yourself as a top priority.

## EXERCISE
### Body Scan

Doing a body scan is simple and only takes a moment, but it can be beneficial if you receive physical, emotional, mental, and possibly spiritual information for you to act on. It can also be used as a starting point when exploring medical intuition, the ability to intuitively diagnose or determine physical or emotional conditions.

**Step 1:** Get yourself into a quiet, comfortable, and relaxed state.

**Step 2:** Take a deep breath in, and then exhale.

**Step 3:** Release any tensions you may be holding in your body. Move or shake your body as needed to accomplish.

**Step 4:** Energetically scan your body with your mind, moving from your head to your feet.

**Step 5:** Notice how you feel. Acknowledge anything uncomfortable and take note of where you feel discomfort or pain.

**Step 6:** Take action to address what shows up that could be of benefit to yourself. This could be stretching, placing your hands on that part of your body and sending energy, or leaning into the discomfort.

**Step 7:** When complete, bring your hands to the top of your head and move them in a downward sweeping motion to smooth out your energy body and release anything necessary back to the earth.

### Alternative Method

If you are in a lot of pain and going into your body seems like it will be too uncomfortable or painful, alter this exercise by scanning your body but noticing all the points where your body is being supported by something. If you are in a chair, notice how the gravity feels pulling on you. Are your legs touching the bed or floor? Notice how it feels. Add anything that can be used to make yourself more comfortable, such as propping your elbows up on a pillow if you are lying down or getting something for your feet to rest on so your core doesn't need to work as hard to support you if your feet don't touch the floor.

Find a neutral place of feeling without pain on your body and focus there to see if you can take some comfort in being aware of a point in your body that doesn't hurt. For example, when I've done this exercise in the past, I noticed my pinky finger touching the table. It felt neutral temperature-wise and wasn't in pain but didn't necessarily feel good either—it just was. Noticing and leaning into that feeling can move your awareness to something small beyond pain and potentially give you even a moment of neutrality and mindfulness.

## The Cauldron of Poesy

In *Magickal Mediumship*, I walk the reader through an energy opening based on the chakra system. I know that this system doesn't resonate with everyone's practices, though it is a part of mine. If a chakra meditation helps ground and center yourself in your body's energy center, by all means use it. I wanted to expand a bit here to another part of my process that is influenced by the Irish bardic poem *The Cauldron of Poesy*, which explores a metaphorical trio of cauldrons we have when we are born. The three cauldrons are the Cauldron of Warming, the Cauldron of Motion, and the Cauldron of Wisdom. To read more about the translation of this poem, read Erynn Rowan Laurie's work cited in the bibliography. Each cauldron is positioned in a different part of the body. The Cauldron of Warming is located within our lower pelvic region and belly. The Cauldron of Motion is located in the center of the chest, where our heart and lungs reside. The Cauldron of Wisdom can be found within our head or sitting on top like a crown.

These cauldrons are spiritual cauldrons that are set up in three different positions when we enter the world. The Cauldron of Warming, the lowest cauldron, is found in the upright position or how we would image a full cauldron to normally be placed, with the opening facing up. This is because we have the basic energies and wisdom we need to live, grow, function, and survive. It is our instincts. However, this is the cauldron that can cause problems by illness or unhealthy decision-making.

The Cauldron of Motion sits tipped over on its side when we are born, meaning that it is partially empty, with the opening facing to the side. It is located near our heart and is where our inspiration resides. It's what catalyzes us; it makes us move. When we do what inspires us and immerse ourselves in our passions, we can tip the cauldron to sit upright. If we deny ourselves of emotions, expression, and exploration, we can feel drained or empty. And if we overdo it, we can feel flooded and unbalanced, which can affect us physically and mentally.

Our last cauldron, the Cauldron of Wisdom, is completely upside down, with the opening downward and empty when we enter the world. The cauldron of the head guides our spiritual development and search for the Divine, higher lessons, and connection. This cauldron can be filled as we find our purpose and integrate wisdom on our path.

## EXERCISE
### Aligning Your Cauldrons

Like taking the time to do a body scan, pausing to feel and sense each of your cauldrons as energy centers can allow you to assess where you stand physically and energetically. This exercise provides some context for where you may want to be focusing your energy.

Take a few deep, grounding breaths. Breathe deep into the center and focus your attention on the Cauldron of Warming in your lower region up to your belly. Notice how your Cauldron of Warming feels. Is this cauldron upright? Is it tipped on its side? Or is it turned completely upside down? How full is your Cauldron of Warming? What is filling it up? Are you taking care of your physical needs? Are you getting enough sleep? How is your relationship to food right now? What nourishes you and fills your Cauldron of Warming? What is the will of the body? Reflect on these questions and remember them as you move to your next cauldron.

Breathe deep into the center and focus your attention on the Cauldron of Motion at your heart in your chest. Notice how your Cauldron of Motion feels. Is this cauldron upright? Is it tipped on its side? Or is it turned completely upside down? How full is your Cauldron of Motion? What is filling it up? Are its contents swirling or still? Are you taking care of your emotional needs? Are you finding joy in everyday moments? What passion are you currently pursuing or does this quest feel blocked in some way? What is the love of the heart? Reflect on these questions and remember them as you move to your next cauldron, the Cauldron of Wisdom.

Breathe deeply into your center and focus your attention on the Cauldron of Wisdom at your head. Notice how your Cauldron of Wisdom feels. Is this cauldron upright? Is it tipped on its side? Or is it turned completely upside down? How full is your Cauldron of Wisdom? What is filling it up? How is your mental health at this time? Do you feel connected to yourself? Do you feel a connection with divinity? What is the wisdom of the head? Reflect on these questions.

Take another deep, grounding breath and return. I always find it helpful to write down what you remember each time you do this to see how it shifts and changes. It can definitely provide direction into where you need to lean in.

## Affirmations and Encouragement

Notice your inner dialogue. How do you speak to yourself? Are you a cheerleader? Are you constantly putting yourself down? If you notice a shift in your inner dialogue, it can be a sign that something is energetically off and needs addressing. To assess the situation, connect with your higher self and ask where the thoughts are sourced. They could be from a type of thoughtform.

As mentioned in an earlier chapter, thoughtforms are energetic manifestations that can influence our physical, emotional, mental, and spiritual well-being. They can occur based on our emotions, thoughts, and beliefs about ourselves or external situations. We know from working with magick that there is power in our words and our thoughts. Our internal world affects the external world. Consider cleansing yourself to remove the thoughtform attached to you or to a situation that may be impacting you. Use affirmations or statements that encourage and support you in your language and self-talk. It takes conscious effort to do this, but it's effective. Replace any thoughts or acts that support self-sabotaging thinking and behavior. When we gain clarity, we start to see what is true, what needs discernment, and what projections and thoughtforms we've created to keep ourselves from seeing what is real.

## Develop a Daily Practice

Having a daily ritual to check in with yourself is simple and easy to do. When I'm feeling off my game, it's often when I've veered from the basics. My process starts in the morning (though it's worth noting that you don't have to like mornings to participate; I'm a night owl, and I still do morning work). Upon waking, I take a few moments to give myself some healing energy. If you know an energetic healing modality (such as Reiki), use it here. It doesn't have to take long, just a few moments to send love and healing while taking some nice deep breaths to start the day off from the heart. During this time, I check in with myself on the goals of the day and notice how I'm feeling. Am I anxious about the day's plan? Is it a leisurely morning that allows me to spend some time reflecting?

I might do the three cauldron alignment and take inventory of my physical, emotional, mental, and spiritual feelings. I check if there is anything I need because sometimes if I'm in a funk, making a note can help. By acknowledging the truth about your feelings, you can highlight a need that may alleviate the issue. I still practice gratitude and intention-setting for my day. It can be done at your magickal altar if you have one or as devotional practice but can also be done while you are brushing your teeth and taking a shower.

### *Daily Ritual Ideas*

- Connect with yourself. Use hands-on healing or send yourself some energy.
- Check in with yourself: How are you feeling, physically, emotionally, and spiritually?
- Practice gratitude. State three things for which you are grateful.
- Set your intentions for the day. What are your goals?
- Align yourself energetically. Use the three cauldrons exercise.
- Cleanse yourself with sacred smoke such as cedar or palo santo or a water or cologne such as rose water or Florida water.
- Sit at your self altar (page 59 for exercise) and connect to yourself. Be open to receiving any messages you might need to hear from your higher self or guides.
- Use a divination tool, such as a pendulum or tarot cards, to seek guidance on your day.

## Scrubs, Salves, and Salts

I enjoy crafting salves, scrubs, and bath salts to keep on hand for when I need them. For example, I reach for the following brain fix salve when I am having a hard time focusing, and it invigorates me. Here are a few of my favorite recipes for enhancing your self-care from body to spirit. I encourage you to try these recipes out and even tweak them according to your needs. Crafting your own blends can be a powerful and effective way to achieve your goals.

### *Brain Fix Salve Recipe*

This is an invigorating blend that can be used for migraines, brain fog, or to spark memory. To use, anoint yourself on pressure points such as wrists, brow, and nape of the neck. This recipe calls for infused olive oils. If you don't have infused oils and are not up for crafting your own, just use plain olive oil as a replacement.

#### You will need

10 drops peppermint essential oil
10 drops rosemary essential oil
20 drops cedarwood essential oil
20 drops lavender essential oil
3 ounces mugwort-infused olive oil
3 ounces St. John's wort–infused olive oil
2 ounces ginkgo-infused olive oil
1.8 ounces beeswax

**Step 1:** Measure out your oil and beeswax.

**Step 2:** Combine oil and beeswax in a double boiler. If you don't have access to a double boiler, you can use a glass bowl placed within a pot of shallow water to create a double boiler.

**Step 3:** Place the mixture on the stove and bring the water to a boil, making sure the water does not get into the oil mixture.

**Step 4:** Stir the oil and beeswax to fully melt them together.

**Step 5:** Once everything is melted, turn off the stove to prevent the oil from getting too hot.

**Step 6:** Add your essential oils. Note: It's important to do this step immediately before pouring. When exposed to heat, essential oils can evaporate, which can weaken the smell of the final product. Time is of the essence.

**Step 7:** Pour your salve into jars or containers.

**Step 8:** Do not move the salves until they are completely set. Once set, you may cap the containers.

### Helpful Tips

- Place a towel or rag underneath where you will be pouring your salves.
- Use a glass measuring cup to do step 7. One trick is to heat the glass measuring cup with hot water so the salve won't solidify when you pour it in. Make sure the glass measuring cup is thoroughly dry before pouring salve into it. Pour your salve mixture into the measuring cup and then into your salve jars.

## *Calm Thyself Bath Salt Recipe*

This is a great recipe for soaking in when you have muscle pain, are feeling drained, or just need to relax. It can also be used when you feel like you need a bit of self-love.

### You will need

1½ cups coarse sea salt
¾ cups Epsom salt
¼ cup baking soda
2 tablespoons rose petals, dried and crumbled
2 tablespoons dried lavender flowers
8 drops lavender essential oil
6 drops rose geranium essential oil

**Step 1:** Mix together the salts and baking soda. Add the dried flowers.

**Step 2:** Slowly and with intention, add the essential oils a few drops at a time. Mix thoroughly as you go if you would like to adjust the amounts of essential oils to your preferences.

**Step 3:** To use, pour 1 to 2 cups of bath salts into the bath while the water is running

### *Eucalyptus Sugar Scrub Recipe*

This recipe creates an invigorating sugar scrub you can use when you need an energy boost or some clarity. It's also lovely to use for sinus issues.

#### You will need

½ cup coconut oil
¼ cup sugar
10 drops eucalyptus essential oil

#### Optional

1 teaspoon vitamin E oil

**Step 1:** This one is simple—take all the listed ingredients and combine.

## Protection Work

Protection is an important and sometimes overlooked aspect of witchcraft. You may think you don't need protection since no one is out to harm you, and that may very well be true. But protection magick is so much more than that. Not only does it protect you from outside forces, negative energy, and harm, it gives you security and defense so that what you do continues without incident or unwanted interference. Here are some suggestions on how to incorporate protection magick in your practice.

### *Wards*

Warding is a form of protection magick that seals unwanted or harmful energies or influences. Some areas of life where you might consider using wards could be on your home, your car, or even yourself. Wards can be chants, prayers, charms, tools, or the assistance of plant, stone, and animal spirit allies. Spirits in general can help provide protection once it is agreed upon or in a contract.

A simple ward is to visualize what you would like protected inside a ball of white light. Set the intention that this white light is to block out all unwanted and harmful energies. This will create a barrier and form an energetic shield. Place black tourmaline in the corners of your home or property to keep away and transmute any ill-intentioned energy that comes in. Crafting a small charm bag and charging it to protect yourself or your space can be very effective. Consider adding plants, stones, or animal curios to your charm, and ask those spirits for protection.

### *Energetic Shields*

The simple method of warding a space by visualizing it in white light to provide protection is a perfect starting place for protection work. In addition to protecting a space, you can ward and protect yourself from unwanted energies by shielding yourself. A simple and easy technique that produces strong results is to envision a shield around you to keep out intrusive and unwanted energies. This shield could be surrounding yourself with white light or the protection of your guides and ancestors. One of my favorite shields is of a rosebush growing around me. It allows in energy that is loving and kind but if the energy changes, the thorns will block it out. Another example is the image of a waterfall that absorbs unwanted energy that is then poured into the earth to be transformed.

## Get Outside

When I go out on a hike or walk in the woods, I will often set the intention to receive a message. If walking in the woods is a challenge physically or geographically for you, go for any walk or even a drive or ride. When I go out with the intention of receiving a message, I look for omens that appear as I walk. Those omens might be an animal that crosses my path, a bird that follows me, the sound of a babbling brook, a certain plant that grabs my attention, or a rock that I find on the path. I don't try hard or make special effort; I just allow what needs to show itself to unfold. I am always amazed at what shows up for me. I've found bones from a spine, which I interpreted as a message that I needed to stand tall and not shrink in the shadow of someone I was dealing with at the time. I have seen foxes playing near me, deer walking in front of me, and even rocks rolling off a small ledge. Sometimes I receive a message that I need to pick up or move something or carry it for a while before returning it. Be open to the messages you receive.

At the same time, be aware of the spirits around you in the woods. Some are friendly, others are indifferent, and still others not friendly at all. There have been times I've heard my name called and instead of following, I booked it home. I know enough from folklore that following the sound of your called name won't always work out in your favor. I've also heard singing and chosen to not engage, as it felt intrusive. Use good discernment about what feels right to do.

CHAPTER 4

# Your Sacred Home

Even when you are not at your best, it's likely that taking care of house and home is still on your priority list. Having a clean space can affect your mind, body, and spirit in a positive way. If you are wanting to foster a healing space for yourself, keeping it clean and maintained is going to pay off. In this section, we'll go over some practical guidance for keeping up with housework as well as some techniques for managing your home's energy.

I should preface this section with the fact I'm a little intense when it comes to cleaning my house. It also feels like an uphill battle. I live in a farmhouse, which naturally gets messy in the blink of an eye. Many animals live in our house as well as in the barn. I also have teenagers and a toddler living with me. And never mind me, who likes to cook and milk the goats! Needless to say, constant cleaning is required, and I'm a little controlling about it, especially when I'm at my best.

However, when I was in the hospital, I had been feeling sick for months, so keeping up with all the tasks was incredibly daunting. I couldn't do it the way I wanted to, which felt defeating. I had to surrender control and let my mother help me. Yes, it was *that* rough. I was lucky enough to have someone willing and able to do this type of help. Sometimes we need to remember to accept help when it is being given or ask for it, like we've talked about already.

There are many techniques for cleansing a home, and this is clearly not a comprehensive list of what can be done. These suggestions are meant to be simple and easier for you (or, if they are agreeable, for community helpers who will help energetically reset and cleanse your space) to accomplish. Doing so creates an environment clear of stuff that could get in the way of having an energetically and physically clean, serene space to promote your healing and recovery needs. And when I say recovery needs, I'm not referring only to after some big health event. Everyone needs recuperation, and folks with chronic and invisible illnesses know all too well the need to recharge. A clean home is a healthy home: the spirits of the home are happier, and I bet you are as well.

## Mundane Ideas for Managing Mess

One of my favorite resources on organizing and cleaning is K. C. Davis's book *How to Keep House While Drowning.* She has great techniques on managing the overwhelm and shame about keeping one's house in order. She also writes the book in a way that makes it easy for neurodivergent folks to easily use it and not need to read it from cover to cover for its benefit. One technique is to keep laundry baskets in all accessible areas. Whether you live alone or with others, you might be familiar with how clothing can magically pile up all over the place. If you have laundry baskets, clothing can be thrown in them to eliminate clutter from the floor or furniture.

Another laundry basket hack Davis suggests is to make sacrificial corner cuts where you can. For me, this was folding laundry. I have employed more laundry baskets for this process. When clothes come out of the dryer, they go into the clean laundry bins for each person. I don't wrinkle them into a ball or anything like that but give them a shake and lay them on top of each other. It reduces wrinkles and takes very little time. If I do smaller loads, I might even skip this part. My sacrifice of completely wrinkle-free clothes is a price I'm willing to pay to keep some of my energy for something else. Finding ways to conserve and even boost my personal reserves is a win.

Besides laundry bins, you can also use more decorative bins for cleaning up on the fly. I'm not saying that you should accumulate a bunch of junk containers, but take notice of where stuff tends to accumulate. I will say that my kitchen is where everyone tends to dump their stuff upon walking in the door. I don't have a perfect solution, but here is one for when I need the space cleared to help with the energy of the space, for my own mental well-being, or if I'm having someone over. If I don't have time to clean the whole place, I place the "unhomed" items in storage cubes or bins, and I suddenly have a decluttered space. I can then return to the bins for sorting or have owners collect their belongings.

## Partnering with Your Home

While mundane hacks for getting your house in order are helpful, it's also incredibly beneficial to get in tune with your living space. Whether you live in an apartment or house, alone or with others, connecting with the spirit of your home is essential. One of the ways I invite folx to start this process is to find an area in your home that feels like the heart. In my house, it's the hearth area, where I have a wood stove. Now, this wood stove currently doesn't work, but it is positioned between the kitchen and the living room, where most of the home's actions take place. I have created an altar to my home as a focal point to commune with the spirits of place. The next exercise shows a way to honor your house spirits, set intentions for the home, and also make a great location for magick related to managing your home's energy.

### EXERCISE
### Home and Hearth Altar

Creating a home and hearth altar is a great addition to your magickal practice. It is a way to invite the spirits of your home to be recognized and honored, and it serves as a focal point for making offerings in exchange for their help and blessings.

#### You will need

A space in your home, ideally in the "heart" of the home (think kitchen or living room)

Candle (any color) to represent hearth fire

Cauldron to represent the hearth

## Optional

Important tools or seasonal items

**Step 1:** Place items you have gathered on your new altar. The candle lends its power and shining light, and it can be a beacon for the spirits that reside in your place. The cauldron has ancestral ties, and its core function is a cooking pot. It provides a vessel to create nourishment for those who dwell in the home. It is a symbol of the hearth itself and provides warmth and comfort.

**Step 2:** If you choose, place other tools and important items on the altar as well. For example, I place some of the tools I use in my practice, such as my mortar and pestle that I use for tea blending. This way, it can be charged upon the home altar, and when I use it, I imbue its blessings and energy into the herbs I'm using. I also have some items from the land and my farm placed there lovingly. These include a small amount of honey from bees, some yarn I have spun from our sheep, some dirt from the front door, and some foxglove petals in a vessel harvested from my garden. I also have an antler, given to me by someone local who found it in the woods, that I have mounted and blessed with a quartz crystal. I also add decor for each season, as this also serves as my focus of honoring the seasons. For example, I harvest local herbs from the land and create a wreath around the cauldron.

**Step 3 (optional):** If it is part of your practice, make sure to leave an empty space for ritual offerings, such as food on small plates or drinks in cups. I make an offering when I cook something special with intention or craft a new tea blend. If I make butter or cheese, I also offer some to the home spirits.

***

Reading about the altar, you may think it's too much to maintain. Well, sometimes it may be, and that is okay. When I have the energy or spoons to keep up with this altar, I make sure to do it. If I don't change it right on time, I don't beat myself up. For example, I don't hold myself to a specific schedule of food offerings. I do it when I have the spoons to make those things and then offer them up.

## Change the Decor, Change the Energy

In addition to having a home and hearth altar, finding ways to spruce up the energy of your space can be helpful for your body, mind, and spirit. If you are chronically ill, chances are you've spent a good chunk of time in your bedroom beyond regular sleeping hours. Speaking for myself, I essentially lived in one room and on my couch for a significant amount of time. And now, if I don't feel well, I go there too. That room has become my safe haven, but it wasn't always.

After I came out of the hospital, my partner and I started the process of getting the house ready for children. It was a good project, as I didn't have to go outside the house (since my immune system was nonexistent). We made changes room by room, and that included my bedroom. We painted, changed the furniture around, and decorated it in a way I had always wanted to decorate. It was a lot of work and lots of the heavy lifting fell to my partner. However, the end result was amazing. Now my bedroom is comfortable.

When we did the same with each room of the house, I finally felt our partnership with the house spirits and that the place reflected us and was our home. I had lived on the farm for thirteen years before it really felt like a space I love.

Don't wait that long to fall in love with your home. Even if it is not a permanent home or you have a contentious living situation like I used to, make a few small changes to bring the space into alignment with you. It could be through aesthetic decoration, using relaxing or energizing colors based on what you need. I went from having a room that I wanted to pump me up and get me out the door to one that really inspired rest and recovery. Play around with ideas starting with mundane factors, and they will affect the energy. Before long, you'll see what you are doing is an act of devotion and self-love. It can be sacred and profound. Once you've got your space set, you can then cleanse and bless it, consecrating it how you see fit.

## *Declutter*

Decluttering is a great starting place if you can manage it. We've already discussed managed mess and how the less you have to clean up, the easier your space is to manage both physically and energetically. Marie Kondo's method of decluttering and clearing space is great if you are able to spend the time and reflect on each piece to see if it brings you joy. In the event you can do this, do it. If you cannot, take sweeps when you can and get rid of what no longer serves you, including your magickal items.

For years, I was a collector of stuff. I had a hard time letting go of the magickal remnants I'd worked on once complete. It wasn't until I was faced with preparing my home for children that I had to buckle down and decide what was really necessary in my practice and what could be stored away, donated, or disposed of in a respectful manner. My magickal repertoire has downsized significantly. Remember that it's okay to add things back after reflecting more on what you actually need.

If you are in your living space and something is bothering you so much that it is problematic, get rid of it. Find the solution or find a way to stop it. Stop fretting on it over and over again. Act on your feeling, because the brain power you gain back feels so good and can truly be used for better things!

## *Creating Comfort*

Creating a visually aesthetic and comfortable space sounds like it shouldn't matter, but it does. Nesting in your home can be incredibly appealing to your mental health and aid the energy of your space to promote healing, recovery, and rest. This doesn't mean you need to feng shui everything perfectly or spend all your money at a home store, but it does mean putting intention into the space you create.

I've found that slightly changing things up with the seasons helps me feel more attuned to the turning of the Wheel of the Year. Creating spaces for rest, such as your couch or bed, with comfortable pillows and blankets benefits you as they are designed to have an inviting atmosphere.

### *Magickal Improvements*

Magickal ways to improve the energy in your home include cleansing with smoke, such as burning a sacred blend of incense. This incense could be store bought (ideally natural instead of synthetic), but use whatever you have that makes you feel good. You could craft your own incense dedicated to making your living space sanctified. You might burn sacred herbs; often the ones you find around your home can be extra powerful for blessing and consecrating your space. Even if you live in an urban environment, you can find "weeds" that are often sacred plants to the witch growing in cracks in the sidewalk or overgrown lots. Some of my favorites include mugwort, mullein, and yarrow.

### *Your Magickal Bathroom*

Depending on your chronic illness, you may also spend a lot of time in the bathroom. Like we discussed with bedrooms, making your bathroom work for you and feel like an energetically supportive and aesthetically pleasing space can make a world of difference. Again, this doesn't mean you need to redo your whole bathroom, but I encourage you to consider color, either with paint or decor that could be relaxing or empowering to you. Create a self-care station for yourself by the bathroom sink that has your hygiene products and also maybe some magickal items. I have my toothbrush, hairbrush, nail polish, some significant makeup I wear frequently (including lipstick and mascara), a large quartz crystal to amplify the energy, a rose quartz, and amethyst for self-love and intuition. These things are arranged nicely in a way I find pleasing. Though it takes up a small space, it brings me some peace when I look at it.

Some other ideas to make your bathroom a sacred space are adding an affirmation you might like to keep close to you. Having foster teens in my home, I have recently added some vintage metal signs that say "Grow Through What You Go Through" and "Be Kind to Yourself." They're good reminders for both them and myself as well.

Whether you use a bathtub or shower, or shower chair, having products that keep you clean and help nourish your body is also an act of self-love.

I have regular soap that I use along with special soaps that I have consecrated for specific purposes, such as "Victory" or "Calm Down." I find scented shampoos and conditioners that have essential oils in them help me relax. If you are someone who responds well to aromatherapy, shower steamers (usually placed on the floor of the shower to make the bathroom smell lovely while the water is running) can have great benefit. If you are taking a bath, you can let the hot water from the sink do the job.

Using or even crafting your own bath salts or soap can be another way to give yourself some love. In the last chapter, I shared a few easy recipes you could incorporate into hygiene routines to make the process more enjoyable. I know there have been times when it's been difficult for me to get motivated for hygiene practices, or it was so physically exhausting that I didn't want to do it. Other times, I was embarrassed because someone needed to help me. Using these sacred soaps or washes helped relieve some of those stressors and made the experience more pleasant than it would have been without.

### *Kitchen Magic Feeding Your Needs*

What are some easy ways to incorporate magick into our kitchen and food? First, using the techniques on energizing your space in the previous section is great for kitchen witchery. You might imbue the words "healing," "delicious food," "healthy meals," "self-love," and "nourishment" into the space. Much like I would add an ingredient into a spell, when I add a spice to what I'm making, I speak to its spirit and ask to borrow its properties for taste and magick: "I call upon the spirit of salt; Mediterranean salt, please lend your flavor to this soup. And as you are tasted, please cleanse and clear and nourish. Thank you for your aid. Blessed be."

I also like to use symbols when stirring something. Try using a pentagram or other power symbols. Another option is using a sigil charged with a certain intent. You can also draw the sigil energetically over the food you are preparing with a finger, your wand, or even your cooking spoon.

At the start of your meal preparation, set your intention. For example: "May this meal be delicious, nutritious, and well received. May all who taste this be nourished and loved. So mote it be."

## EXERCISE
### Empowering Your Space with Words and Symbols

Imbuing your space with words, sacred symbols, or sigils is also a way to consecrate the energy in your home. Power symbols like those in the Reiki tradition, elemental pentagrams, or self-created sigils are great, but you can even energetically write your intentions into the room. You could use words like "healing," "power," "peace," or "calm." These simple techniques can bring about real shifts and I encourage you to try them.

**Step 1:** Ground and center yourself in your space. Take a few deep, grounding breaths. Imagine your feet have roots growing out of them that go down into the earth. Feel that energy return up through the roots into your body. Imagine you have branches growing out of your shoulders and head that twist up into the sky. Feel the energy from the sky move down the branches into your body. Feel the energies of earth and sky combine within you. You feel grounded and centered.

**Step 2:** Taking your dominant index finger, write out the word "healing" in the air and feel the energy of this word expand into the space.

**Step 3:** Use your dominant hand to push that energy and word into the room. Feel it expand and fill the space.

## Self Altar

Something I heard author and witch Devin Hunter speak about in a presentation inspired something I've been doing for many years now: creating an altar to yourself. Give yourself the freedom to imagine you are a spirit or deity. If someone was going to create an altar devoted to you, what would it look like? What would be placed on it to honor you? A picture? Items that are important to you? What corresponding stones, plants, and curios align with you? What offering could be left for your favor or intercession? Once you've contemplated these questions, build something with that information.

Once you have a working altar to honor yourself, you can use it to connect with your highest self, honor your own spirit, charge your items, and send healing to and from yourself. I leave a wooden bowl on my self altar that I put my magickally charged jewelry in when I'm not wearing it so it can continue to be connected with me.

### *Days of Celebrating You*

Auspicious days for your self can be celebrated at this altar. Obviously, your birthday is meant to celebrate you, but you also may feel planetary alignment, moon cycles, or even seasons associated with your constitution. You may also observe special days of celebration by doing self-care. For example, I always try to take a late September or early fall day just for myself. I take myself out to get a fancy coffee and go on an adventure, just me. Doing this helps me stay in touch with who I am and lets me have a sense of freedom and play. I will often go on a walk or foliage drive to see the autumn leaves.

### *Offerings of Plants and Stones*

Another way to access and work with your self altar is when you are feeling unwell. I have magickally charged stones for certain ailments (covered in a later section) from which I pick a few to keep by my bed or on my person, depending on how sick I am feeling. I also have lotions I've crafted that smell nice and corresponds with herbs that benefit the typical ailments I have. For example, arnica is good for arthritis, so I keep some arnica cream on my altar. I also have a lotion I crafted with magickal intention that has peppermint and lavender, which sometimes is helpful for my migraines.

More energetically related altar pieces I include are blue kyanite, one of my favorite stones. I find when I hold it and focus on my breathing, it helps realign my energy if I'm off. I have a large heart-shaped lepidolite, which contains lithium, that I take out when I am feeling particularly depressed and will sleep with next to my head. I also have a sleep charm that I keep there if it is not under my pillow or on my bedside table.

### *Candle Offerings*

Another regular offering I make to myself is candles. I am a scented candle connoisseur and, to me, the candle feels like it is lighting my way; it relaxes me, and the scent helps make the space feel sacred. I also enjoy lighting particular incense—usually it's lavender, but I indulge my inner teenager from time to time and pull out the nag champa. I recommend finding triggers like these that will help put you at ease at your altar and in your personal space.

### *Other Offerings*

When I am having rough times health- or otherwise, I make offerings to myself at the self altar. These are often self-care items or foods that nourish me and "feed" my spirit, made the same as any other spirit offering. In the past this has included fancy cheeses, dark chocolate, lavender cookies, honeycrisp apples, red wine, handcrafted tea blends, lattes, candied ginger, cucumbers, or whatever else I enjoy that is special to me. I leave these on the altar, but unlike other spirit offerings where I let a spirit receive the energy and then ritually dispose of leftovers without eating or sharing in what was offered, I let myself eat the treats on my altar—after all, they are for me!

## EXERCISE
## Build and Bless a Self Altar

Now that we've walked through how to use a self altar, along with some ideas for making it work, here is a ritual to put yours in place.

#### You will need

A picture of yourself that you like or a mirror that you can gaze at

Pieces or representations of accomplishments or what makes you special; it could be awards, resumes, and other items that remind you of who you are and what you have already accomplished.

Corresponding stones, herbs, or animal representations significant to you

*__Note:__ Refrain from including other spirits that you work with on your altar—this is specifically dedicated to you

Offerings for yourself: Choose things you enjoy that are consumable or tokens that can stay on the altar

Altar cloth, if you choose to use one

**Step 1:** Select a location for your altar. Choose a place that you are frequently in, such as your bedroom, your office, or a small area like a writing desk or bookshelf (if you love books).

**Step 2:** Cleanse the space. Use sacred smoke, a cleansing spray, a wash, or a sacred oil to cleanse and clear the space to be worked on.

**Step 3:** Place your items on the altar space. Consider putting down an altar cloth in your favorite color or material. In the center of your altar, place your image or the mirror. Then decorate the altar with your meaningful items until it is pleasing to you.

**Step 4:** Consecrate the altar in your name. Speak from your heart your intention for the altar. You could say something like the following:

*I consecrate and bless this altar*
*to be a sacred space where I honor myself.*
*May I hear and clearly know my highest and wisest self.*
*May I be empowered by any and all work accomplished here*
*for the highest healing good. So mote it be.*

**Step 5:** Your altar is ready to be used. Connect with yourself at it daily. I know daily practices can be scary for chronically ill folx, but I encourage you to at least take a moment each day to look at yourself or in the mirror, pull a card for guidance, or use the altar as a touchstone for making magick happen in your life. Your altar is a source of power for you—feed it, and it feeds you.

## Practices for Your Self Altar

It's helpful to visit your self altar regularly (daily if possible, though we've discussed pacing and spoon theory, so plan your energy accordingly). I don't find working with my altar to be draining. If anything, it can be a kind moment for myself even during an exhausting day. It's also a great place to say affirmations and speak aloud daily intentions. I have an oracle deck and tarot deck I kept on my altar. I ask the oracle deck what I need to focus on for the day and draw a card of the day from the tarot deck. I leave these cards out all day so I might see them as I pass by. Having daily divination with low pressure isn't daunting at all for me, and I enjoy it. If anything feels like a chore for you, don't do it. Use divination at your altar when you feel you need it.

You also may wish to incorporate this altar into your rituals and magickal work for many purposes. In the following exercise, I outline a ritual to empower yourself at your self altar. However, the ritual structure can be used for any type of ritual you would like to perform at this altar. Under the "Work" section of the ritual, substitute the spell or working you would like to accomplish, and then follow the remaining ritual structure.

## EXERCISE
### Ritual for Empowerment

Before you begin the ritual process, prepare yourself for the work. Make sure you know how your space is oriented. Where is east, for example? Make sure you know which directions the quarters are located in. In the Temple of Witchcraft, the element of fire is in the east and air is in the south, so I write my rituals this way. If you prefer a different orientation, please adjust for this.

#### You will need

Bowl of water
Small amount of salt
Incense such as frankincense or copal
Self altar with mirror or picture of self

#### Optional

Wand

#### Preparing for Ritual

Check in with all parts of yourself and do a body scan. Then walk through the process of aligning your cauldrons. Add salt to the bowl of water.

Starting in the north, dip your fingers in the salt water and sprinkle around the circle. Say aloud: *I cleanse this space by earth and water.*

Light the incense and walk around the circle starting in the north, wafting the smoke to cleanse the space. Say aloud: *I cleanse this space by fire and air.*

### Casting the Circle

With the altar in front of you, raise your wand or use your dominant hand. Move around the circle in a clockwise manner while saying aloud:

*I cast this circle to protect us from harm on all levels,*
*I consecrate this circle to allow only the most perfect*
*energies in and to block out all others.*
*I charge this circle to be a space beyond space,*
*a time beyond time, a temple of perfect love and perfect trust.*
*Where only the highest will reigns sovereign.*
*So mote it be!*

### Calling the Quarters

Call the quarters in a clockwise manner. Start by facing north. Raise your left hand and call:

*To the north, I call upon Great Stag and the element of earth. Please guard and guide us in this circle. Hail and welcome.*

Face east. Raise your left hand and call:

*To the east, I call upon Mighty Horse and the element of fire. Please guard and guide us in this circle. Hail and welcome.*

Face south. Raise your left hand and call:

*To the south, I call upon Wise Crow and the element of air. Please guard and guide us in this circle. Hail and welcome.*

Face west. Raise your left hand and call:

*To the west we call upon Changing Snake and the element of water. Please guard and guide us in this circle. Hail and welcome.*

### Calling the Guides and Allies and Setting Intention

Facing your altar, state aloud:

*I call upon the Goddess, God, Great Spirit.*
*I call to my guides and I call to the angels,*
*I call to the Ascended Masters and I call upon the Mighty Dead.*
*I call to the Hidden Company,*
*the witches who have walked this path before me.*
*I invite you to guide and guard me in the space as I do my work*
*I call upon the ancestors, I call to the beloved dead.*
*I call upon those of my own who are healthy, well, and able in Spirit,*
*Oversee this rite and may it be for my highest healing good,*
*harming none.*
*So mote it be.*

### The Work

Gaze into the mirror or at the picture of yourself on your altar. Allow any feelings that surface in you to bubble up. Notice how you feel about how you look. Then notice how you feel about yourself overall. Notice how you feel about your illness(es). Continue gazing into the mirror. When you feel ready, speak from your core to yourself. State aloud:

*I recognize myself as a divine spark.*
*I recognize the unique beauty I hold.*
*I am strong, secure, empowered, and healing,*
*And am far more powerful than ever told.*

### Raising the Energy

In a sweeping motion, gather up the energy with your hands. When you've collected the energy, push the energy up and out of the circle with the extended sounds of "E-A-O" (pronounced "ee-ah-oh"). Then place your hands across your chest to ground the work in yourself or place your hands on the ground to send some energy back to the earth.

### Release the Guides and Allies

Facing your altar, say aloud:

*I thank and release the Goddess, God, Great Spirit.*
*I thank and release my guides and the angels.*
*I send thanks to the Ascended Masters and the Mighty Dead.*
*I send thanks to the Hidden Company,*
*the witches who have walked this path before me.*
*I send thanks to the ancestors and to the*
*beloved dead who gathered here.*
*Thank you for overseeing this rite,*
*and may it be for my highest healing good, harming none.*
*So mote it be.*

### Release the Quarters

Release the quarters counterclockwise with your right hand raised, starting in the north and then moving west. At each cardinal point, say loud:

*To the north, I thank and release the Great Stag and the element of earth. Thank you for guiding and guarding us in this circle. Hail and farewell.*

*To the west, I thank and release Changing Snake and the element of water. Thank you for guiding and guarding us in this circle. Hail and farewell.*

*To the south, I thank and release Wise Crow and the element of air. Thank you for guiding and guarding us in this circle. Hail and farewell.*

*To the east, I thank and release Mighty Horse and the element of fire. Thank you for guiding and guarding us in this circle. Hail and farewell.*

### Closing the Circle

Moving counterclockwise with your wand or dominant hand raised, say aloud:

*I cast this circle out into the cosmos as a sign of my work. The circle is open but unbroken. So mote it be!*

# PART TWO
# Opening to the Magick

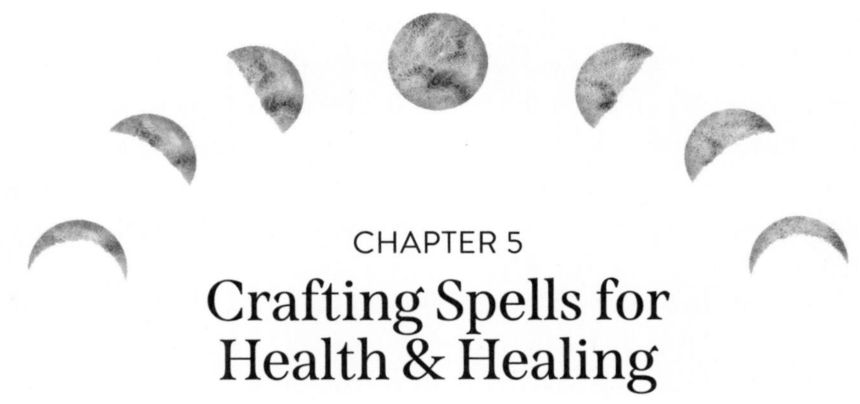

CHAPTER 5

# Crafting Spells for Health & Healing

What is a spell? Spells are a focused way for us to direct our intention using our will. There isn't a wrong way to do a spell, but a successful spell is one that works or works better than you had hoped. There can be more effective ways to cast spells or enact your magic. What follows in this chapter is by no means exhaustive. I'm hoping to give you some ideas that you can then take and modify and create more spells as you see fit. It's a smattering of what has worked well for me, and I hope it works well for you.

Some things of note before you start your spells. When considering what you want to accomplish, really sit with it. Don't just jump right to "I need money… boom—green candle spell!" Think about what kind of job you want, how many hours you want to work a week, what kind of culture you want your workplace to have, what kind of room for advancement would you prefer, what kind of leadership team would be best, etc. Get really into it! The key is to be specific in what you want but remain flexible so that what you manifest is this *or better* when it happens.

Now is the time to craft your spell. We'll explore some options that I enjoy working with in my practice. You might consider a petition spell, sigil magick, crafting a charm bag, creating a doll, or candle magick or a combination for your work. I often blend a few techniques together, but simple is also a totally viable path. Most of what we'll discuss are types of sympathetic magic, where like produces like. When we use plants, stones, and beyond in our magick, whatever corresponds with these ingredients lends itself to what we are trying to accomplish. Contagious magick is another type of magick in which things that have been in contact can continue to have an effect on each other, like with doll magick. Something made in our likeness that possesses something of ours (like hair) will continue to affect us as we do work on it.

Once you have your goal and are decided on what kind of spell to cast, you perform the spell—but then what? You need to act on it to make it happen. Doors may be provided, but to achieve momentum toward getting what you need, you must walk through the door. Any good spell needs follow-up and real-world action. Don't forget this important step!

## Ritual

The idea of doing a ritual may seem daunting when you are already low in supply of spoons. It's easy to feel overwhelmed or too low-energy and decide to do nothing. I am here to encourage and remind you that doing anything is better than nothing. Injecting a sense of the sacred into your daily routines will give you the feeling (as well as the benefit) of having done something. You don't have to make big, elaborate gestures or ritual performance art, though if you are able to, I recommend giving it a go. Mixing the sacred with mundane is effective. When you read about the following ideas for magick, just know that everything is adaptable; adjust whatever you'd like to make it work for you.

No matter your approach, crafting good rituals can help you achieve success with your spells. Being mindful of correspondences and elements such as timing, color, and spellcraft techniques can make even the simple powerful. Rituals that are simple or elaborate can both be effective, but I find the most effective ones involve heightening your energy to a state beyond the ordinary. Taking yourself out of everyday consciousness (most commonly through meditative or ecstatic means) leads to bypassing your subconscious mind to make you feel the magick, which is part of how it becomes real. Magick is personal, and finding out how to elevate your mind to that state turns up the juice. Music is effective for me, so a lot of my magick involves listening to loud music or singing. I may not jump up and down but summoning breath to sing, even if it's not pretty, even if it's not as supported as when I am well, even if my voice cracks—it moves me and therefore moves my magick. Likewise, getting into a meditative, out-of-the-ordinary, calm, centered, and collected mindspace makes a difference.

## Magickal Timing

Magickal timing takes advantage of specific lunar, astrological, and planetary times to harness their corresponding energies in a spell or ritual. Working in tandem with the moon, sun, and planets lends their attributes to the workings you are doing. Working with the heavenly bodies' energy can boost your results, and I recommend exploring their use. Here are some jumping-off ideas for working with magickal timing.

### *Lunar Cycles*

The moon and her ever-changing phases connect us to the tides and lunar mysteries. Understanding the moon's phases is a good starting point if you are less familiar with magickal timing. By looking into the night sky, you can get an idea of what phase the moon is in and how it may affect your mundane and magickal goings-on. Following the lunar cycle and harnessing the energies as it waxes and wanes can enhance your spellcraft and spiritual practices. The dark moon and waning energies may be better for reflective and contemplative work. The moon is considered waning after the full moon peaks and begins to grow in darkness. Waning moon magick is for banishing and removing energies. When the moon is waxing and gaining light or is full, it can be used to gain things in your life or to manifest something.

Using waning spell magick to reduce or diminish common afflictions that go hand in hand with chronic illness can yield successful results. For example, you may wish to banish or lessen symptoms, remove obstacles in the way of your health, or reduce or eliminate side effects from medications.

## *Astrological Energy*

Working with astrological energies is a common practice in witchcraft. In addition to the lunar phases, you could look to see what sign the Moon is in to add a boost of correspondences to your work. You could also harness the energy of astrological influences when the Sun or another planet you wish to work with is in a particular sign. Here are the signs' corresponding energies that could work in your magick.

***Aries*** is ruled by the planet Mars. Body parts ruled by Aries include the head, skull, hair, teeth, and blood. Aries is a cardinal fire sign, and its archetype is the warrior. Keywords include action, force, and protection.

***Taurus*** is ruled by the planet Venus. Body parts ruled by Taurus include the neck, throat, ears, sinuses, and thyroid. Taurus is a cardinal earth sign, and its archetype is the steward. Keywords include embodied, strength, physical, luxury, comfort, and pleasure.

***Gemini*** is ruled by the planet Mercury. Body parts ruled by Gemini include upper body parts in pairs including arms, shoulders, hands, and lungs. Gemini is a cardinal air sign, and its archetype is the trickster. Keywords include intelligence, cunning, adaptable, creative, and technological.

***Cancer*** is ruled by the Moon. Body parts ruled by Cancer include the breasts, stomach, biologically female reproductive system, and the lymphatic system. Cancer is a mutable water sign, and its archetype is the mother. Keywords include nourishing, empathetic, emotional, receptive, and caregiver.

***Leo*** is ruled by the Sun. Body parts ruled by Leo include the heart and back. Leo is a mutable fire sign, and its archetype is the artisan. Keywords include loyalty, artistic, passionate, and prosperous.

***Virgo*** is ruled by the planet Mercury. Body parts ruled by Virgo include the digestive system and pancreas. Virgo is a mutable earth sign, and its archetype is the healer. Keywords include healing, meticulous, efficient, and inquisitive.

***Libra*** is ruled by the planet Venus. Body parts ruled by Libra include the kidneys, bladder, and lower back. Libra is a mutable air sign, and its archetype is the judge. Keywords include equality, balance, observation, and mediation.

***Scorpio*** is ruled by Mars and Pluto. Body parts ruled by Scorpio include the genitals, colon, rectum, and urinary system. Scorpio is a fixed water sign, and its archetype is the guardian. Keywords include secretive, taboo, gatekeeper, betwixt, and instigator.

***Sagittarius*** is ruled by the planet Jupiter. Body parts ruled by Sagittarius include the liver, hips, and thighs. Sagittarius is a fixed fire sign, and its archetype is the teacher. Keywords include visionary, guide, and teacher.

***Capricorn*** is ruled by the planet Saturn. Body parts ruled by Capricorn include the bones, joints, knees, spleen, ligaments, tendons, and skin. Capricorn is a fixed earth sign, and its archetype is the father. Keywords include authoritative, diligent, and stable.

***Aquarius*** is ruled by the planets Saturn and Uranus. Body parts ruled by Aquarius include the lower legs and ankles. Aquarius is a fixed air sign, and its archetype is the rebel. Keywords include unique, humanitarian, innovator, and oppositional.

***Pisces*** is ruled by the planets Jupiter and Neptune. Body parts ruled by Pisces include the feet and pituitary and pineal glands. Pisces is a fixed water sign, and its archetype is the ecstatic. Keywords include evocative, psychic, escapism, and devoted.

## *Planetary Days*

The English days of the week were named after the planets and their corresponding Roman and Anglo-Saxon gods. Working with the planetary energies of the day is a good way to notice patterns and begin incorporating their uses into your life. Here is a list of the planets by day and some of their basic correspondences.

***Sun—Sunday:*** Health, wealth, success, joy, optimism, healing, luck

***Moon—Monday:*** Psychic ability, divination, spirituality

***Mars—Tuesday:*** Strength, vitality, health, sex, anger, passion, will, protection, aggression, strategy, masculinity

***Mercury—Wednesday:*** Magick, knowledge, communication, writing, speech, technology, administrative tasks

***Jupiter—Thursday:*** Luck, expansion, prosperity, money, victory, beneficence, health, growth

***Venus—Friday:*** Love, friendship, relationships, compassion, beauty, art, nature, femininity, self-care, empathy

***Saturn—Saturday:*** Work, stability, constriction, attention, reversals, endings, death, ancestral connections, past lives, karma, maleficence, boundaries, diminishment

### *Planetary Hours*

Along with days, magickal timing also includes the seven classical planets' rulership over hours or parts of the day. Using planetary hours in combination with planetary days allows you to work with multiple planetary energies at once. The hours follow a sequence called the Chaldean order: Saturn, Jupiter, Mars, the Sun, Venus, Mercury, and the Moon. The order is based on the pattern of slowest- to fastest-moving planets as they appear in the night sky and, traditionally, the farthest to nearest planets relative to Earth.

Each day includes twenty-four divisions, or hours, based on the patterns of light and darkness. The first hour of the day begins when the sun rises and is ruled by the planetary day's ruler. So the first hour of Sunday starting with sunrise, is the hour of the Sun. On Monday, the first hour is ruled by the moon; on Tuesday, the first hour is ruled by Mars; and so on, based on the day's planet. The hour before each sunrise is ruled by the planet that comes before the day's ruler, so just before dawn on Monday is an hour of Mercury. You can calculate the planetary hours by dividing the amount of time from sunrise to sunset in minutes by twelve to give you a planetary unit for the day.

For example, if the sun rises at 6:00 a.m. and sets at 7:00 p.m., you would divide the daylight into twelve parts of sixty-five minutes each and then night (from 7:00 p.m. until the next sunrise—around 6:00 a.m.) into another twelve parts of about fifty-five minutes each. Finally, you assign the planetary rulers in order, beginning with the ruler of the day. This may seem like a lot of work. Fortunately, there are several smartphone apps and websites that can automatically do the calculations for you.

Here are the keyword associations for the planetary hours.

***Saturn:*** If you are wanting to diminish, constrict, or banish something, Saturn is a good advocate.

***Jupiter:*** Work with Jupiter's energy if you are wanting to gain something. Jupiter is associated with expansion, growth, healing, prosperity, good fortune, and miracles.

***Mars:*** If you need power, work with Mars energy.

***Sun:*** For all general health, the Sun can be a powerful ally. The Sun is good for optimism, hope, confidence, luck, and sense of self.

***Venus:*** If you are taking a self-care day or need to nurture yourself, work with Venus for magickal timing.

***Mercury:*** If you need to communicate with a medical provider or appointment scheduling, call on a Wednesday or in the hour of Mercury. Mercury has an affinity for transactional communication and expression.

***Moon:*** The moon is a great ally for spirit work and spellcraft, and working with lunar cycles is a good way to engage with the moon.

To take this another step further, mix planetary days with the planetary hours. For example, if you are trying to get into a doctor's office earlier than the waitlist's wait time, call on a Wednesday in the hour of the Sun.

## Color in Healing and Spellcraft

Color associations are helpful additions to your magick and healing. The more resonance your magick has that's aligned with your goal, the more energy it lends to the spell. I primarily use color with candles but it can also work with clothing, stones, and more. Here is a list of colors and their spiritual associations.

### *White*

White is often associated with spirituality, purity, devotionals, memorials, spirit contact, blessings, healing, and cleansing. It is also a universal candle color for all workings. This color is sometimes connected to the Moon. Use it in spells related to healing and purification and to connect with spirit guides.

### *Red*

Red is connected to love, passion, power, romance, affection, energy, lust, fertility, attention, libido, sexuality, strength, determination, will, desire, motion, fire, anger, war, and primal energy. Red's planetary association is Mars. Body associations with red include matters of blood, metabolism, and respiration. Red can increase blood pressure and respiration rate. Use it in spells when you are using the Power and Attraction Oil.

### *Purple*

Purple corresponds to psychic ability, victory, command, compulsion, control, mastery, ambition, and prophetic dreams. One of purple's planetary connections is Jupiter. Use this color in spells where you are optimistic about something happening, when you would like a clear path to victory, or to have success with a medical procedure.

### *Green*

Green relates to matters of growth, healing, money, wealth, prosperity, luck, gambling, fertility, business success, matters of the heart. Green is associated with the planet Venus. Bodily associations with green include a calming and healing effect: it can slow metabolism, respiration rate and pulse, and reduce blood pressure. It is connected to reproductive matters and matters of the heart. Green is considered beneficial to all matters of the mind and body. Use it for any spells having to do with healing.

### *Yellow*

The color yellow is associated with optimism, mental agility, confidence, clarity, communication, fast action, success, happiness, money, legal matters, friendship, excelling at school, and wisdom. Yellow is connected to internal organs, especially the liver and muscular systems. It is also associated with the Sun. Use it in spells where you are hoping for a good outcome, positive news, or clarity on a situation.

### *Blue*

Blue is associated with health, expansion, peace, communication, clarity, harmony, abundance, protection, and love. Blue is helpful for mental health and emotional needs. Blue helps self-expression as well as matters related to the throat. This color and purple are associated with the planet Jupiter. Use it in spells when you require protection, a peaceful outcome, or need to be heard (including by a medical provider).

### *Black*

Black is helpful for matters of protection, repelling negativity, banishing, bringing harm, destruction, cursing, enemy tricks, hexes, jinxes, and coercive magic, or it can be used universally. Black's planetary association is Saturn. Use it in spells for protection, reducing side effects from medication, and diminishing something health-wise (for example, reducing inflammation or growths).

### *Orange*

Orange's correspondences include recognition, control, changing plans, creativity, removing obstacles, opening paths for new opportunities, communication, and cunning. Orange is associated with the reproductive organs. Orange can also help with matters of the cardiovascular system, digestion, and increases in appetite and immunity. Orange (and brown) can be associated with Mercury. Use it in spells to open the way for a health care appointment or communicating with a health provider.

### *Brown*

The color brown is associated with practical and material things, blessings, legal matters, animals, and neutrality. Brown is sometimes seen as a warming color that provides comfort and stability. This color and orange are associated with the planet Mercury. Use it in spells to aid in work and legal matters related to your benefits or health.

### *Pink*

Pink is connected to drawing love, success, friendship, romance, attraction, and gentleness. Pink can help with accepting sustenance and nourishment physically and emotionally. Pink can be associated with the planet Venus, though green is Venus's traditional color. Use it in spells to find connection with others in your shoes or good medical providers.

## Candle Magick

Another type of working that can range from simple to more creative is candle magick. Keeping magick simple, especially if you are not feeling 100 percent, can still produce effective results. Working with candles, oil lamps, or a flame to accompany prayer is recognized by most religions. These light- and heat-giving items have a rich history of being used for offerings or to call for the intercession of spirits, saints, and deities. Working with candles in magick can help transmute your intention when used with a petition spell.

To begin with candle magick, choose a color that matches the intention of your working or petition. The associations beginning on page 74 under "Color in Healing and Spellcraft" often feature in candle magick in choosing which color candle to use. However, magick is a personal practice, so use what you are guided to use or simply what you have. And if you aren't sure which color to use, white is great for all workings.

There are many types of candles available to use in spells. These can be simple chime candles, candles that are shaped into an image, freestanding candles, or enclosed candles. If you are pairing your candle magick with a petition, once you have drafted your petition, you can follow the same instructions but instead of lighting your petition on fire and burning it, you may choose to place it under the candle you are charging for this request.

I often hold and charge the candle with my intention before lighting it. You may consider other additions to your candle working. If you are working with herbs, stones, and allies, you could add them to the candle or place them nearby to amplify its effect. I often dress a candle with a magickal oil and either roll the candle in herbs or load the candle with oil and herbs. Dressing a candle is similar to anointing. As you would anoint a person with oil to prepare for a magickal working, you would dress a candle.

If the candle is freestanding and my spellwork involves bringing something to me, I dress the candle with oil in motions toward myself. I would dress the candle in the opposite direction if the goal was to remove something. After the candle has been dressed, you can roll it in herbs that correspond to the magick at hand. If I'm using multiple herbs, I thank each plant spirit, one by one.

Once complete, I roll my candle to imbue it with their energies. If you are working with a glass-enclosed candle, poke three or five holes in the top (I employ a screwdriver for this job) into which you can add a small amount of magickal oil to imbue the candle with its properties. Use only a small amount—three drops in each hole will do it. Any excess you may spread over the top of the candle. Tracing a symbol of power or moving in directions corresponding with your request is appropriate. You may also add a small amount of herbs to the candle.

If you add anything to any candle, do not overload it: the herbs catch fire and could potentially explode in the glass. It is wise to never leave your candles unattended and to keep them in a firesafe container or space. When you have completed dressing and blessing your candle, you are ready to light it. Light the candle while stating your intention or after the petition has been stated and placed beneath the candle.

## EXERCISE
### Be Nice Boss Spell

For those who have chronic illnesses, the workplace can sometimes be challenging. With appointments and sick time, leadership's or management's favor can sometimes worsen, even if your cause for absences or reduced work is just. If you are looking to influence your boss in your favor, here's one idea to do so. As this spell is targeting a specific individual or individuals and not you, be sure it's *truly* what you're willing and that you wish to do it.

### You will need

A candle shaped like a skull
A plate or container for the spell
Something to inscribe a name on the candle
Angelica root for protection and empowerment, especially for all women
Calamus root to take control of the situation
Cinquefoil to reach out and seize that which you are hoping to accomplish
Licorice root to assert your dominance in the situation
Rosemary to lend power and mind influence
Sugar to sweeten the intended target

**Step 1:** Write the name of the person or persons or department you wish to influence on the skull candle. Place the skull candle in the center of the plate or container.

**Step 2:** One by one, place each herb in the shape of an arrow pointing toward the skull. Speak aloud to each herb as you do so, asking it to lend the noted energies to your spell.

**For example:** "Angelica, I thank you for your support and aid in this rite. Lend me your protective and empowering energies so that I may be successful in my endeavors. May I rise in power over (name targets) and assert my will. May there always be peace between us. Blessed be."

**Step 3:** Light the candle and state, "I name this candle to be called (name of target) in the likeness of (name of target). May they hear and act upon my will. So mote it be." Whisper to the skull candle what you wish to have dominance and control over in the situation. Act as if you are speaking to the actual person or persons targeted. Whisper the thoughts and ideas you wish to enter their minds. Do this nightly for seven days or until the candle has burned out.

## EXERCISE
## Spell for Finding the Right Medical Support

One of the ways I've worked to draw the most helpful and knowledgeable team of professionals to me is the following spell. You can use this to attract one particular medical professional or to assemble your own support team.

### You will need

A white seven-day candle
A screwdriver or something to make holes in the candle
A red permanent marker

**Optional Step:** You might consider crafting a sigil or writing a petition with this spell.

**Step 1:** Using the screwdriver, create three holes in the seven-day candle.

**Step 2:** Using the red marker, draw a thick red cross on the glass surrounding candle.

**Step 3:** Next, draw a caduceus on the glass candle.

**Step 4:** Add three drops of Power and Attraction Oil into the holes. Power and Attraction Oil is best used to attract something to you (recipe on page 80). The herbs and oils in the recipe correspond to drawing things toward yourself and amplify that process with power.

**Step 5:** State aloud your intentions in the form of a petition. For an example, see page 81 in the section on petitions.

**Step 6:** Use the triangle of manifestation hand gesture to bless and imbue the candle. To make this gesture, touch your thumbs and pointer fingers together with your palms flat to form a triangle-shaped window. Then use the triangle of manifestation to bless and consecrate the candle three times. Draw the triangle up to your brow, then down over the candle each time.

**Step 7:** State aloud, "So mote it be!"

## EXERCISE
### Power and Attraction Oil Recipe

Power and Attraction Oil is used to amplify power and attract what you want. It has many purposes and is used frequently throughout this book. The following recipe is based on a folk magic blend I was taught.

#### You will need

15 milliliter glass container/bottle with secure top
1 drop milliliter cinnamon essential oil: heats things up and makes things happen fast
1.5 milliliter frankincense essential oil: amplifies the recipe's power
1.0 milliliter orange essential oil: Cleanses and adds luck
12 milliliters jojoba oil
Lovage root: draws your desires toward you
Orange peel: luck
Cinquefoil: anything five fingers can do, five-finger grass can do for you
Lodestone: magnetizes and attracts

Combine the essential oils into a glass container or bottle with a secure top. Thank each of the spirits of the plants, resins, and stones for partnering with you in this oil blend. Add small pieces of lovage root, orange peel, and cinquefoil (also called five-finger grass), and the lodestone to the bottle. Fill the remaining space in the container with jojoba oil. Shake the container. Always be sure to test a small amount of oil on the skin to make sure you don't have a reaction.

## Petition Magick

Petitions are a simple and effective way to craft spells to manifest or banish something in your life. In Christopher Penczak's *The Casting of Spells*, he sums up the formula for petition spells, specifying that the elements key to producing results are announcement, evocation, intent, conditions, and gratitude.[8]

8. Christopher Penczak, *The Casting of Spells: Creating a Magickal Life through the Words of True Will* (Salem, NH: Copper Cauldron Publishing, 2016), 79.

The **announcement** is the proclamation of who you are, so it is clear whom the spell is intended for.

The **evocation** is the calling of spirits, powers, and divinities to appear and be present for your working. It establishes the open connection for the power you wish to work with for your spell.

The **intent** is the request or declaration of what you wish to accomplish. It is best if you spell this out as clearly and precisely as possible. Be direct, and put as much feeling and will into this portion as you can.

The **conditions** of the spell are the clauses around your intention. These are important and sort of like fail-safe clauses. The classic example is trying to manifest money: without conditions, you could achieve this goal but someone you love might die and you would be left with inheritance. There were probably better ways to manifest that money! Some good stipulations to consider adding include "for the highest good, harming none" or "for the good of all involved."

The last component to a good petition spell is **gratitude**. Being thankful for your spell as if it has already happened lends power to it. It is as important to express your gratitude for those who lent a hand in the doing as it is to act as if it has already happened. Thankfulness is a generally helpful mindset to have that can provide benefit to the spellcaster.

Here is an example of a petition spell for finding a new health care provider.

> *I, Danielle Dionne, ask in the name of the Goddess, God, and Great Spirit, under the watchful eyes of the ancestors, to grant me a new hematologist who will be knowledgeable, empathetic, and within my health network. I thank the Goddess, God, Great Spirit, and the ancestors for all favors and boons and ask that this be accomplished in the next moon cycle and for the good of all involved, harming none. So mote it be!*

I've had good luck with petition spells in many situations, including successful procedures and swift recovery for others who have been in health crises. I find my success is due to clear intentions and strong will focused into the work.

## EXERCISE
## Glamour(ish) Petition Spell

With chronic illness, we certainly aren't looking our best everyday. If you need to pull it together by looking and feeling your best for an event or outing, here's a candle magick spell that can help beautify, empower, and cast a glamour so that you stand out as beautiful, vibrant, and strong to anyone who sees you. I have used a similar working when I've had to present something and wasn't at my best, and it helped significantly. Try it as is or modify as you see fit for your needs.

### You will need

Cinnamon to spice things up and be perceived as at your best
Rosemary for beauty and empowerment
Cinquefoil to reach out and seize that which you are hoping to accomplish
Rose petals for beauty and sensuality
Chamomile for power and luck
A pink, red, or white candle
A plate or contained surface to place candle and herbs on
A square piece of paper and a pen

**Step 1:** Cleanse yourself energetically and physically. Ideally, this spell should be done after a shower and before you apply makeup (if you plan to). Take your time, and relax into the shower. Use your favorite soaps or body products—the more luxurious, the better.

**Step 2:** Consider casting a circle or creating sacred space. It is not necessary, but I find it is often beneficial to do so for petition work.

**Step 3:** Write your intentions onto the piece of paper. It could look something like this:

> *I, (name), ask in the name of the Goddess, God, and Great Spirit that I may look and feel my best at (name of the event). Let all who gaze upon me recognize my strength, stamina, power, and beauty. May my illness go undetected, and may I be as symptom-free as possible at this time. May*

*this be done for the highest good, harming none. Thank you for your blessings and support. May there always be peace between us. So mote it be.*

**Step 4:** Place the candle in the middle of your plate or container.

**Step 5:** Place a small amount of each herb in a circle around the candle. Speak to each herb and ask it for its support in this spell. You can use the herb reasons listed to make this part more personalized to each plant. For example: "Cinnamon, I thank you for your support and aid in this rite. Lend me your heat so that I may be energized and sparkle at this event. Help me spice things up for my highest healing good. May there always be peace between us. Blessed be."

**Step 6:** Once all herbs are on the plate, read aloud your petition spell over the candle. Declare your intentions and light the candle. Place the petition paper under the candle. Gaze at the flame and feel it empowering you. If you have a safe place to let it burn while you attend the event, do so. If not, let the candle burn while you continue getting ready.

## Doll Magick

Another form of magick that could be employed for healing benefit is doll magick. Dolls, effigies, poppets, and items made in someone's likeness are commonly used in witchcraft. These can be used for healing or hexing the target. Some of my great successes in healing myself and having blessing bestowed on me have employed effigies. I like crafting humanoid figures from air-drying clay. My preferred method for crafting these is to create a shape representing myself or another person I'd like to work magick on and then carving out a hollow space in the back where I can "load" or add magickal items such as plants, roots, stones, bones, or other items that correspond with the work I am doing. I will do this in a ritualized style, and once I've charged the items by speaking to them aloud, I place them in the back of the doll. I seal the doll with more clay. I then go through a process of baptizing or naming the doll in my name or after the person I wish to work on.

## Sigil Magick

Sigil magick is another simple and effective process that can be used to achieve your intention. Sigils are magickal symbols designed to represent an intention or an idea. You can create them to look simplistic or express your desire in a more artistic form. As with most spells, the first step is to determine your "why." Once you know what you wish to accomplish and have spent time ruminating on the specifics you wish to achieve, it's time to craft a clarifying statement. The statement can be succinct, but it's helpful to hold the energy of everything you are putting into this spell with you as you do this work.

For example, if you would like a job that is accommodating to your health and well-being needs, you might craft that as a statement. As you design this sigil, visualize that job. You might speak aloud all the intentions that you have for this job you came up with, and I recommend adding "for my highest healing good" or "I ask for this or better" at the end. Including this clause is a good idea, as you may not know what is truly in your best interest or what you may be locking in to the deal.

There are many ways to craft a sigil, but I still use the way I was initially taught. Take the letters of your clarified statement and eliminate the vowels. Then delete any duplicated letters. Next, use your creativity to craft a symbol using the remaining letters. You can use sigils crafted by others, but I find it is more effective to create your own. If you are going to use another person's sigil, make sure you understand what went into crafting it. Otherwise, you don't truly know what you are using in your magick.

Once you have your sigil, you can use it in your spell.

**Accommodating new job**

**CCMMDTNGNWJB**

**DTGWJB**

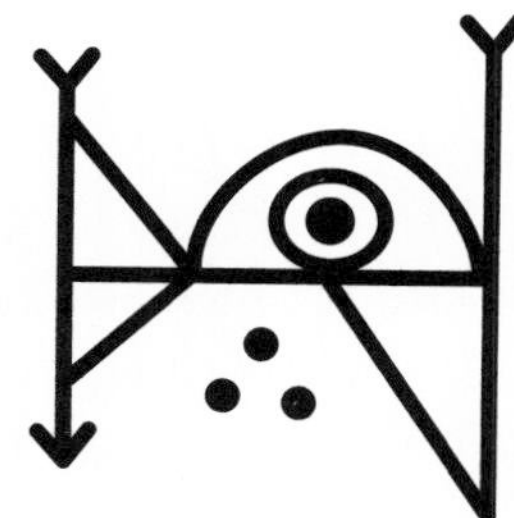

Sigil Accommodating New Job

## EXERCISE
## Invisibility Sigil Spell

Sometimes it's not in our best interest to share information about our chronic illness with someone. If you want your illness to be undetected and concealed, or if you just want to go unnoticed or under the radar, try this spell for invisibility and protection.

### You will need

Agar-agar, a type of seaweed; it can be bought it in powdered form, as it is used as a thickener in food and beverages
A small bag or container
Paper or parchment to craft a sigil

**Step 1:** Using the sigil magic covered in this chapter, craft a sigil using the words "Invisible Illness" or another statement about what you would like to accomplish with this working, such as, "Undetected Illness," "Not Noticed," or "Overlook My Illness" if you feel those are more appropriate.

**Invisible Illness**

**NVSBL**

With these letters, craft your sigil and write it on a piece of parchment.

**Step 2:** Hold the agar-agar powder in your hand. Speak to the spirit of the plant in the powder you are holding. Ask the plant spirit to partner with you for invisibility. Tell it why you wish to do this and the circumstances around the situation.

**Step 3:** When complete, state the intent:

> *With this agar-agar and sigil crafted, my illness is now invisible to (name whom you would like to be protected from). I am protected from their gaze and actions. May I be left in peace. So mote it be.*

## Craft Healing Charms

Crafting charms is one of my favorite acts of magick. Charms can take many forms and can be made of anything you desire. A charm could be a handcrafted item made of paper, clay, stone, plant material, or a combination. It could be a type of cloth satchel or an enchanted piece of jewelry used for a purpose. It can be stealthily and easily concealed, for example by using a mundane object that has been magickally consecrated with purpose.

### EXERCISE
### Power and Stamina Charm Bag

Here's an example of how to craft a charm to boost your energy and provide more stamina to get you through your tough days.

#### You will need

Cedar, palo santo, or other sacred smoke

Offerings for yourself—these could be a scented candle or frankincense incense

A square of cloth; three inches square works well. Any cloth will do, but if it's cut from a piece of your clothing, even better. You could also include color correspondences, but it's completely up to you.

A small piece of petition paper and a pen

An herb for energy boosting and reinvigoration, such as ashwagandha, coffee beans, peppermint, or rosemary

A bone and animal curio from a strong creature, such as horsehair

A stone for power and endurance, such as red jasper or bloodstone

Power and Attraction Oil (recipe on page 80)

A string to tie the bag

**Step 1:** First, cleanse yourself and the space you will be working in with sacred smoke such as cedar or palo santo. Do this by wafting the smoke over your body in a sweeping motion. If you are able, craft your charm at your self altar or in front of it. Make offerings to yourself as you feel appropriate. Light a scented candle or perhaps some frankincense incense (for power) while doing this working.

**Step 2:** If you have specific spirits that you work with, call to them from your heart. It can be as simple as saying:

*I call to Goddess, God, Great Spirit. I call to my guides and guardians.*
*I call to the ancestors and beloved dead,*
*those who have walked the path before me.*
*I honor you and seek your aid.*
*Be present with me in this work.*
*So mote it be.*

**Step 3:** Lay the cloth before you. If you want this charm to work just for you, write your name in the middle of the piece of paper. Then write out the petition, intention, or purpose of your charm bag around your name. You could use the following statement or write out what comes to you.

*May this charm grant me strength, stamina, endurance, and power to get me through my days for the highest good, harming none.*

**Step 4:** Anoint the four corners of the petition paper and its center with Power and Attraction Oil.

**Step 5:** Fold the paper toward you, rotate, and repeat until you have folded the paper three times.

**Step 6:** Place the paper in the center of your square cloth. Add the following items to your charm, holding each one in your hand and speaking out loud to it. Hold it close to your mouth; as you speak the words, your breath should flow to it. Add the herb and speak to the guardian plant spirit ally. (This example uses ashwagandha.)

*Ashwagandha, rooted in the spirit world, I ask for your blessings in this charm. May you assist me with balance and strength. Help me be adaptable and powerful as I go about my days. Thank you for your aid. I honor you.*

Add the animal component or bone. (This example uses horsehair.) Say:

*Cunning and wise animal spirit ally, Horse, I ask for your blessings in this charm. Lend me your strength and endurance throughout my days. Thank you for your aid. I honor you.*

Add the stone (in this case, red jasper) and say:

*Stone ally of power and endurance, Red Jasper, I ask for your blessings in this charm. Lend me your power so that I may be empowered throughout my days. Thank you for your aid. I honor you.*

**Step 7:** After adding all the items, anoint the four corners and center of the pile with the oil.

**Step 8:** Gather the cloth from the corners and tie the string around it to seal the charm. Tie three knots and state:

*This charm is mine and now alive. As I have willed it, so mote it be.*

Keep this charm on your person or on your self altar. You can charge this charm on your altar and continue to apply the oil you used while stating the charm's purpose to reenergize it. This can be done as often as you see fit, such as weekly on Sundays or Tuesdays or during the full moon.

## Visualization Spells

We've covered some great basics for spellcrafting. However, all these methods require stamina and energy to create—what about when you just aren't able to do all the necessary steps? This is where visualization can be a useful tool. If you are not someone capable of seeing images in your mind, speaking aloud what others might visualize can be effective. In fact, speaking out loud adds power from your voice and brings it into being, so consider using your voice if you have the strength. There might be times your practice needs to revolve around less "stuff" and more mental will. You could visualize the steps you would do as a magickal act.

For example, you could use the following incantation on its own or maybe pair it with doll magick or a candle spell. If you are bedridden and can't do the actual crafting of the doll or candle working, you can envision choosing a blue candle for healing and then imagine you are adding frankincense essential oil for amplification or the Power and Attraction Oil to help ensure a successful outcome that attracts the results you want. You might see yourself in your mind's eye adding cinquefoil (five-finger grass) to the candle, as this herb has resonance with what hands can do; in this case, it could aid and guide a steady surgeon's hand. You might add catnip to the candle in your vision to help calm and soothe nerves. As you do this, feel what it feels like to take each step.

Visualization is also useful when you are sick and have trouble maintaining your offerings for spirits. While it's best to make offerings and keep up your end of the bargain for your spirit contracts, I've found my spirits are open and amicable when I have done visualizations of their offerings when I truly couldn't have done it otherwise. I have even offered up items that I couldn't have afforded at the time, showing them what I could offer as well as what I think they should have. Use your mental will, the power of voice, and ingenuity. These can be powerful and effective tools to use when you may be feeling powerless.

## EXERCISE
### Successful Surgery Spell

Here is a simple incantation spell that can be used if you are heading into surgery. This could be used on its own or paired with doll magick, a candle magick spell, or the visualization discussed earlier.

*May the surgeon's hands be steady,*
*May their minds and tools be sharp.*
*May the procedure go smoothly*
*With no complications or infections.*
*And may recovery be swift and easy.*

*I trust in the Goddess and God's Hands.*
*So mote it be!*

## EXERCISE
### Healing Visualization Spell

Here is a quick little spell incantation that could be used alone or be paired with another type of magick or visualization.

*Rise up, healing serpents, and wrap around me*
*By flower, stone, and bone,*
*Heal what ails thee.*

## EXERCISE
### Spoon Spell

One spell I've incorporated into my practice is a spell for having enough spoons (see page 11 on spoon theory). I paired this spell with my personal altar and doll working. All this spell requires is spoons. I used small coffee spoons I found online that were in the shape of flowers. You can use whatever spoons you have available (no pun intended) to place them on an altar space for this working.

**Step 1:** On the evening of the full moon, leave the spoons out and say: "May these spoons be charged by the full moon. May they provide more spoons and energy when I most need them. So mote it be."

**Step 2:** Before the sun rises, bring them back in the house and store them until you need them.

**Step 3:** If you are having a difficult day or are feeling frazzled and lacking spoons, retrieve a spoon from where they are stored and add one or two to your altar. Say, "I ask that these spoons provide me with more spoons. May I use this extra boost of energy for my highest healing good. So mote it be."

**Step 4:** Repeat this every full moon to recharge your spoons.

***

**One last tip:** In the spirit of sustainable magic, challenge yourself to minimize spell waste whenever possible. Seek innovative and environmentally friendly ways to practice your craft, fostering a harmonious connection with the natural world.

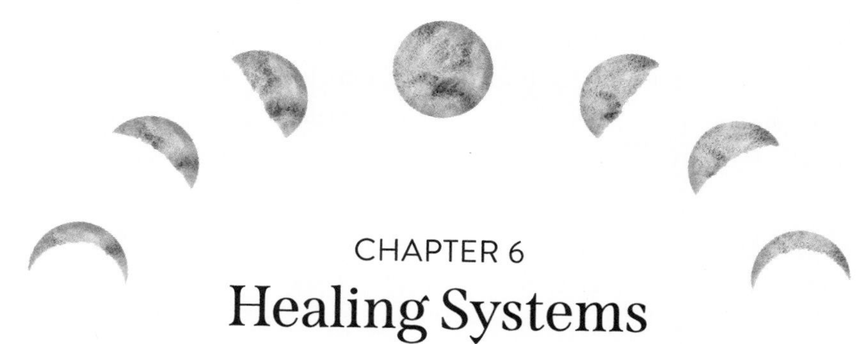

# CHAPTER 6
# Healing Systems

This chapter covers types of healing modalities that you may feel called to explore on your healing journey. Exploring might include receiving these types of healing or even learning how to do them so you can use them on yourself or others.

When I was in high school, I worked at a pet store. I met a woman who was volunteering to do animal communication sessions. After talking with her a bit, I found out she also practiced Animal Reiki. She would go on to be my first Reiki teacher for levels I and II. I was seventeen years old when I learned how to be a Usui Reiki practitioner. When I was twenty-one years old, I spent more than a year studying with my Reiki Master Teacher until I was attuned to be a Reiki Master Teacher. I also studied and practiced Karuna Reiki, Animal Reiki, Shamanic Reiki, and Shangri-La Reiki, each different systems mostly founded in Usui Reiki. I've had profound experiences of healing for myself and witnessing that of others. For several years, I ran Animal Reiki healing groups as well as Reiki shares for my community.

There are other forms of hands-on healing or energy healing systems such as Integrative Energy Healing, crystal healing, shamanic healing techniques, and many other types of healing. Learning about healing modalities has helped me understand the body's energy better and also develop my own integrated healing methods.

## Unlocking the Ability to Heal Ourselves

I'm very much of the mindset that we can unlock our own healing abilities and resources when facilitated by healing practitioners. I do not think I have the power to "heal" others, but I am certainly able to help provide healing energies to promote balance and restoration and activate others' ability to heal. Your body knows best and will do the rest to its best ability. This is why both having a healing practitioner to work with on your health challenges and doing your own self-healing can be a powerful combo.

When I first learned Reiki I and II, it was not expressed to me how important it can be to do self-healing. All my focus was on the other. For years, I did Reiki for others and never focused on myself. When I began to study with my Reiki Master Teacher, she assigned me the task to do work on self-healing every day. It's something that has stuck with me in my personal practice, and I do my best to incorporate it every day. First thing in the morning, before I put my feet on the floor, I give myself a few minutes of Reiki. I put my hands on my heart and belly, take a few grounding breaths, set my intentions for the day, and let the Reiki flow. It doesn't have to take a long time, just a moment or so. It's a kind way to start the day without expending a lot of resources—if anything, it provides more.

I also like to give myself Reiki at the end of the day when I fall asleep. Over the past few years, especially with illness and toddler life, I admittedly hit the pillow hard and fell asleep before finishing this process, though I don't beat myself up about it. If I am having a hard time falling asleep, it can be nice to soothe myself with some hands-on healing energy.

When searching for a healing practitioner to partner with, look for someone whose energy blends well with your own. That doesn't mean you need to be friends or community members, but it's important to feel at ease with them. I often get nervous and must consider my medical PTSD, so it's essential that I find someone who can take care of me and my needs, reassure me, and whom I find trustworthy while I am on the healing table. Just like with spells to find the right medical professionals, I can also use magick to find the right healing practitioner.

## Reiki

Most people are familiar with Reiki or have at least bumped up against it at some point. Reiki is a Japanese system of energy healing founded on the revelation and understanding of the body's energy system. Reiki practitioners strive to improve health and quality of life by offering Reiki energy and restoring balance. Reiki is used in self-care and care for others, and it is offered in private practice and in hospitals and medical settings as an adjunct and supportive therapy to wellness and traditional medical care. The form of Reiki that many people practice today, Usui Reiki, has been in use for over one hundred years.

Reiki can be traced back to Japan in the early twentieth century, when Dr. Mikao Usui rediscovered it. Usui was a Buddhist practitioner searching for a healing method to address physical ailments and promote spiritual growth and well-being. His journey took him to Mount Kurama, a sacred mountain near Kyoto, where he embarked on a twenty-one-day meditation and fasting retreat. During his time on the mountain, Dr. Usui received spiritual revelation in the form of three miracles. He was struck by a powerful energy flowing through him, leading him to be enlightened about Reiki healing and its symbols. Reiki translates to universal life force energy with *rei* meaning "universal" and *ki* meaning "energy."

Dr. Usui's healing abilities and spiritual insights formed the basis of Reiki as a holistic healing system. He began teaching this method to others, including Chujiro Hayashi, a naval officer, and Hawayo Takata, a Japanese American woman who brought Reiki to the Western world. Reiki involves the practitioner channeling this universal life force energy through their hands to promote relaxation, balance, and healing in the recipient. Over the years, Reiki has evolved and branched out into various forms and traditions, and it is still being expanded upon today. At its core, Reiki remains a practice rooted in the belief that by tapping into the universal energy, individuals can facilitate physical, emotional, and spiritual healing and growth. Reiki has gained widespread popularity and acceptance as a complementary therapy that offers a gentle and non-invasive approach to holistic well-being.[9]

If you haven't experienced Reiki before, I recommend giving it a go. It's so commonplace now that you likely have a Reiki practitioner local to you and can book a session with them. Or look for Reiki shares, in which attendants look for guests to participate in exchange for new practitioner feedback. For years, I attended community Reiki shares and found it beneficial to receive Reiki and also experience what it was like to provide Reiki to folx from many walks of life with a vast number of ailments.

### *Hands-On Healing*

Across traditions and cultures, hands-on healing methods provide ways of sending healing energy to those who need it. But even outside of any tradition, you can use hands-on healing as an effective way to transfer healing energy. The key to remember is that you are not sending your own energy into the person—you need a source. Whatever your belief structure or source of power resonates, use it. That could be asking a deity to help send healing through you, working with energy from the earth and sky, or working with a healing guide. You want to make sure you are not depleting yourself at the cost of healing someone else. Allow the healing to flow *through* you and not *from* you.

## Integrated Energy Therapy (IET)

Integrated Energy Therapy is another healing modality I have been trained in and found beneficial on my healing path. I mostly incorporate processes that I learned through my training here into my own version of healing that I call Integrative Energy Healing. It is not one form but instead blends what I've learned through my training and traditions into something unique that will work for each recipient. While not all traditions encourage blending modalities (and I respect that), Integrated Energy Therapy encourages adding it as a complementary modality to other healing techniques. I find this very valuable.

9. International Association of Reiki Practitioners, accessed January 18, 2024, www.iarp.org.

Integrated Energy Therapy (IET) was developed at the Center of Being by Stevan J. Thayer. One of the catchphrases about IET is that it "gets the issues out of your tissues." IET can aid in the release of suppressed feelings and limiting cellular memories. Overall, it supports you in enhancing your health, life purpose, prosperity and creativity. It is an empowering healing modality that supports your experience fulfilling loving relationships in all areas of your life.

IET uses what is called the violet angelic energy ray, which is brought to us through angelic guides to work with our spiritual DNA. According to the Learn IET website, they chose the term "Integrated" to convey their vision of "integrating the pain of the past, into the power of the present, to bring about the joy of the future."[10] IET is a helpful energy therapy practice on its own, and it also makes a wonderful complement to other holistic techniques such as massage, Reiki, and Therapeutic Touch. While IET is a perfect standalone energy therapy system, it is ideal to integrate IET into sessions based on other holistic modalities as well as integrate the techniques of other holistic modalities into IET sessions.

## Shamanic Healing

Core shamanic healing practices have been incredibly empowering and healing for me on my path, both when I have practiced with other people for their own healing and when I have had it done for myself. Some of my most profound healing experiences have been shamanic healings.

The shaman may serve by removing energies that are inappropriately present or by returning energies that have been lost. This includes soul recovery to accomplish healing via the return of lost parts of the soul.

When it comes to learning about core shamanism and healing, it's important to find the right teachers and be culturally mindful about whom you are learning from, how, and what. I would consider looking into the works of Sandra Ingerman and Michael and Sandra Harner. Dr. Daniel Foor's book *Ancestral Medicine* and his other works are another excellent resource for culturally mindful ways to work with the dead.

10. "What is Integrated Energy Therapy® (IET®)?" accessed January 22, 2024, www.learniet.com.

## Meditation

I bring up meditation because it's often listed as something folx with chronic illness and pain should try to do to help with physical pain as well as to calm the mind. Sometimes we forget how important and effective the basics can be. If I find myself off track, gently redirecting my focus to the minimal and easy things to do can often give me more bang for my buck than going big.

"Meditation" is an umbrella term for practices in which an individual uses techniques such as mindfulness or focuses the mind on a particular object, thought, or activity to ultimately achieve a clearer mental and emotional state. Meditation is often one of the most common suggestions because it has been shown to reduce stress, anxiety, depression, and pain as well as enhance a sense of peace and well-being. If you struggle to meditate by focusing on something, it may be helpful to listen to a guided imagery meditation. These can be listened to wherever you stream music or even on YouTube.

If I am having pain, one of the practices that has helped me even in public is to shift my focus to the pain. Using it as the focal point allows me to notice and become aware of it and eventually move through it. Sometimes I do this at the beginning of a meditation when I intend to do something else but the pain is too much for me to focus on something else. This technique can get me through that barrier, allowing me to continue with my original meditation focus.

## Visualization

If you do not have the means to learn any of the previously discussed healing traditions and techniques, that doesn't mean you are unable to work with healing energy. Visualizing what you want to happen can be an effective healing tool. In your mind's eye, envision the receipient healing: broken bones are mended, rashes or bruises fade to normal skin color, blood cells become whole and functional, and so on. Whatever malady is afflicting you or the person you are sending healing energy to, visualize what it looks like for them to be well.

Another technique to promote healing is to visualize yourself or the person who would like to receive healing in colorful lights. Consider sending green or purple (both considered healing colors) light to your recipient. Or send whatever you feel represents the healing color they need.

### *Aura Healing*

Another form of healing using color is healing the aura. If you are doing a body scan on yourself or applying it to another person, you might notice colors in their aura or over parts of their body. Their color and shape can be indicative of what is going on with them physically or energetically. You might see gray-colored areas or places where it seems too bright or dull or faded. You might see holes or tatters in their auric field. Visualizing the repairs and sending color to those weakened spots can be healing. And the information gathered from where the colors need to be sent may give you some information on health issues in body, mind, or spirit.

## EXERCISE
## Healing Colors

In this exercise, you will explore how it feels to fill the auric field with individual colors. This is a great grounding technique that also familiarizes you with the process itself for times when you want to fill your energetic field with a color to ease and heal something you are feeling.

**Step 1:** Sit in a comfortable position, ideally with your spine straight. Make any accommodations you need to be able to move through this exercise in comfort. You want to be free from focusing on your discomfort so you can pay attention to this experience.

**Step 2:** Take three deep, centering breaths. Inhale, exhale. Inhale, exhale. Inhale, exhale.

**Step 3:** Begin to sense the energy field, like an engulfing egg shape around your entire being. Sense and perceive what it feels like to become aware of your energy.

**Step 4:** Take another deep breath in and out. This time, as your inhale, feel the energy of your aura fill with the color red. Notice how you feel. Breathe out, filling your aura with the color red. Repeat this deep breathing for a few moments. Feel your energy being imbued with strength, determination, passion, and love for self and others.

**Step 5:** Repeat this process with the following colors:

***Orange energy:*** Feel your energy being imbued with creativity and inspiration

***Yellow energy:*** Feel your energy being imbued with vitality and confidence

***Green energy:*** Feel your energy being imbued with healing wisdom

***Blue energy:*** Feel your energy being imbued with a sense of calm and peace

***Purple energy:*** Feel your energy being imbued with intuition and psychic awareness

***White energy:*** Feel your energy being imbued with purifying light

**Step 6:** When you have completed all the colors, become aware again of your normal energy field around your body. Take a deep breath in and exhale. Bring your awareness back to the room. When you are ready, open your eyes.

CHAPTER 7

# Divination for Support

Learning a divination system is invaluable if you are facing health issues. Divination provides clarity and insight into questions or situations of interest. Divination is the process of using a method to predict or receive guidance. When it comes to having lots of medical situations, having a process for checking in with your body, medications, treatment, and outcomes is useful. Divination is of great benefit for those seeking to enhance their psychic ability or partnership with spirits.

Daily divinations are part of my personal practice, and they provide guidance into the scope of my day. They're useful as a way of checking in on any pressing situations or questions. If I already have a gut feeling about something, I feel more prepared if my divination backs me up. If I am getting responses that counter my intuitive feelings, divination gives me pause to feel further into the scenario in case there's more I need to know. I recommend finding a system that resonates with you and working with it.

Some divination systems that I work with are only for me, and some systems I use are for work exclusively with specific spirits who help me connect to their energy current. I have card decks that I work with for client readings and my own personal sets. Ultimately, your work is unique to you, so explore what calls you.

Let's walk through some divination techniques that may be helpful for you to explore as you seek what works best for you. When doing a divination, it's appropriate to ask for how you would like the information to be conveyed to you. Here's an example of a simple blessing you could do prior to divination: "I ask for the highest and best guidance to be shown to me at this time. I ask that I may be in harmony with this guidance and understand all messages given to me."

## Pendulums

Pendulums are a great starter divination tool across the board. This simple divination method consists of a weight hanging from a cord or chain. The direction in which the weight swings determines a "yes" or "no" response and can be used to work with a spirit or the operator's higher self. The spirit or higher self subtly influences the pendulum or its holder to indicate the appropriate response.

There are many ways a pendulum could be helpful in healing. I often use my pendulum to divine which flower essence or energetic healing would be most helpful at this time. Sometimes I use a pendulum when working on a healing client to see if any of their energy centers need attention. I also do a pendulum divination when I'm wondering if I should attend an event. If I do not feel well that day but need to RSVP to something, I'd rather get a heads-up if I am likely to go or not. This also goes for day-of plans to help gauge if I am feeling well enough to stay for the entirety of the event.

### EXERCISE
### Using a Pendulum

Here is a simple exercise to learn to use a pendulum. The more you work with your pendulum, the more comfortable you will be connecting to it and trusting its use.

#### You will need

A pendulum

**Step 1:** Hold the pendulum in your dominant hand. Either hold the end of the pendulum or let the chain hang over your finger while holding the end with your thumb.

**Step 2:** While the pendulum is still and not moving, ask it to show you what "yes" looks like. The pendulum will begin to move to show you what "yes" looks like. The motion could be side to side, front to back, or clockwise or counterclockwise.

**Step 3:** Stop the pendulum from moving. While the pendulum is still, ask it to show you what "no" looks like. The pendulum will begin to move and show you what "no" looks like.

**Step 4:** Now that you know yes and no, you may begin asking your divination questions. When you are done, thank your pendulum for its assistance.

**Step 5:** It's helpful to cleanse your pendulum before and after use or on a regular basis.

## Muscle Testing

Muscle testing is another go-to for my on-the-fly divinations. Muscle testing is a form of applied kinesiology and is used to measure bodily responses to various substances. It is a way to tap into the subconscious and innate wisdom of the body. Muscle response is measured by applying slight force. Typically, weakness indicates a "no" response while strength indicates a "yes" response. There are multiple ways to muscle test, but the way I often use is making an O-shaped ring with my pointer finger and thumb on one hand. I link my other pointer finger and thumb around the ring. I ask a question and then test to see if I can break the link.

Like the pendulum, muscle testing is useful for determining if I will be well enough to attend an event or commit to booking sessions when I may not be 100 percent. I also use it when choosing herbs and stones to work with for healing. I have even used muscle testing when I was having an allergic reaction to a medication but didn't know it at the time. It has helped me trust my body more and be in tune with it. I began to feel unwell after being prescribed some antibiotics and was on the fence about whether it was something or nothing. I decided to ask if I should get my blood checked (which is how I know if I am relapsing) and soon found out I was indeed having a reaction that caused my blood to go wonky and required a hospital visit.

## Cartomancy

Cartomancy is divination using a deck of cards that includes tarot cards, standard playing cards, and oracle cards. Cards may be assigned specific meanings or interpreted by the reader. Cards are a good beginner tool as they can provide yes or no answers in addition to more nuanced guidance and interpretation. Cartomancy is one of the most widely used forms of divination and can be easily picked up and partnered with if you are wanting to devote a deck to a specific purpose or spirit. There are healing decks available that may be of use for checking in with your body. I am a fan of Laura Tempest Zakroff's deck, Anatomy of a Witch Oracle: Cards for Body, Mind, and Spirit.

## Cleromancy

Cleromancy is a form of divination using the casting of lots. It could be throwing bones, the *I-Ching*, divination with dice and runes, or even working with crystals. I work with several forms of cleromancy in my personal practices, such casting my bone set that includes bones as well as objects and trinkets as signifiers. This is a more spirit-led interpretive practice for me. I also roll dice that has been consecrated to get specific answers like yes or no in varying degrees. Both interpretive and yes or no systems can be a beneficial form of divination for health. You could potentially craft your own system with items that are sacred to you that represent certain aspects of your illness, well-being, and overall health.

## Automatic Writing

Automatic writing allows the unconscious mind to open as a channel for spirits, including spirits of disease or medication, or the highest and wisest self. It can be used to bring through yes and no answers as well as messages with more context. While it is possible to be aware of what is being written while it is occurring, sometimes it is completely unconscious. Sit with the intention of connecting to a spirit of your highest and wisest self while holding a pen to paper. Let yourself get into the flow and write or draw messages that come through related to health and healing. It can also be used to check in with your mind, body, and spirit. Messages received in this way often get to the core of what may be going on or give you new perspective on a situation.

## Scrying

Scrying is the art of gazing into a medium form with the intent of seeing a vision or gaining insight. The medium form could be a black mirror, a crystal, or even a body of water. Scrying has a long tradition as a divination tool. It can provide personal guidance and inspiration and be used for prophecy or to conjure the images of spirits. Scrying can be helpful in answering questions about health and healing too. For example, while scrying you may ask to see how you feel on a particular day or time. You may clairvoyantly see images that can be interrupted, but your other psychic faculties may also perk up. Sometimes you might see something while scrying and also feel something in your body that corresponds to what you are seeing. Experiment and see what presents itself to you.

## Iridology

Iridology is divination through the eye's iris. Iridology or iridiagnosis is a technique that looks at the patterns, colors, and characteristics in the eye. It considers the eyes the windows into the body's health. This is often used to figure out a patient's systemic health situation. Iridology uses iris charts to determine what parts of the iris correspond with which parts of the human body. Iridologists can determine what areas of the body are in a distressed state (for example, overactive or inflamed) and use this information to identify past, current, and possible future health issues. I've only had a few experiences with iridology but they were spot on.

***

These divination systems are only a sampling of what's out there. Find what resonates with you to gain clarity and insight. You could create your own versions or even invent whole systems. You may find some work well for personal divination and others are better for connecting to specific guides or spirits.

## Coping with Bad Readings

Divination can be a wonderful tool providing accurate insight into healing and well-being. But what do you do when the guidance you receive is less than optimistic? First, consider the source. Was it a reading that you provided for yourself? Are you feeling clearly about the reading? If so, keep in mind that the reading is based on the current energies of where things are right now. You might consider asking follow-up questions like "Is there anything I can do to change this outcome?" Even if the answer is no, sometimes having a heads-up regarding the trajectory of something can be helpful. It will reduce the shock when you actually experience that low point, and it lets you create some back-up plans beforehand.

For example, after I was hospitalized for my blood disorder, I vowed to be a one-and-done case where I'd never again need to be hospitalized for it—although this is a possibility, it is much rarer than the majority of cases. I received a reading that told me otherwise. It made me upset, but it also helped me come to terms with the fact that I needed to plan on sometimes being in the hospital for treatment and to pay attention to my blood draws. As things turned out, I was readmitted. Even though that was a blow, it had been softened by knowing it was likely to happen at some point again anyway.

CHAPTER 8

# Magick for Empowerment

When you have chronic illness, you lose a lot of control in your life. You are at the mercy of your illness, your job, your health care team, the entire health care system, and beyond. I'm sure many of you, like me, have seen your share of challenges. One area of my life that I continue to focus on is my mind. Sometimes it's the only thing I have control over, and it doesn't even feel like I have *that* some days. Magick provides ways to combat doubt and empower yourself as you push through the hard times and do your best to stay as well as you can. Looking for ways to empower yourself and doing the work pays off. In this chapter, we'll look at techniques that can reap rewards if you put in the effort.

## Working with Your Shadow

"Shadow work" has become somewhat of a buzzword these days. In the witchcraft community, there is a lot of discussion on shadow work, though I think we sometimes miss the mark on what that work actually entails. Shadow work takes energy and practice but is well worth incorporating into your spiritual work. At its core, it is about working with your unconscious mind to uncover the parts of yourself that you repress and hide from yourself, including trauma or parts of your personality that you subconsciously consider undesirable.[11] Where there is light, a shadow is also cast. We all have pieces of us that may be lurking in the background that we don't want to acknowledge and try to shut out. The goal of working with your shadow is to develop self-awareness and get to a point of self-acceptance and compassion. This can be achieved by becoming acquainted with the parts of yourself through your spiritual practice but often is best accompanied with therapy.

In the third year of the Temple of Witchcraft's Mystery School, students are made to keep a shadow journey for the year. You record your thoughts and feelings that arise during the entire year for different categories like shame, anger, fear, guilt, jealousy, and resentment. At the end, during the shadow initiation ritual, the journal is burned. This was one of the most profound experiences I've had in ritual. I highly encourage you to do this or something similar, while making sure you have the support necessary to process what comes up for you.

## EXERCISE
### Shadow Journaling

Journaling is a great jumping off point to explore shadow work and there are many workbooks now available to help prompt your shadow exploration. Journaling helps process emotions and release them. It can be a meditative practice unto itself. It can lead to self-discovery and uncover your true feelings. Please note, this practice can bring up a lot of stuff, so it's best done in conjunction with the support of a therapist.

#### You will need

A journal explicitly for this purpose, ideally one that can be completely burned; if not, one that you can rip the pages from when it is time to burn it

Pen

Lighter and fireproof container or firepit

11. Christopher Penczak, *The Temple of Shamanic Witchcraft: Shadows, Spirits, and the Healing Journey* (St. Paul, MN: Llewellyn Publishing, 2004), 67.

**Step 1:** Determine how long you would like to keep a shadow journal. You might choose to do this exercise over a week, a month, or even a year.

**Step 2:** Each time you write in your journal, pick a selected amount of time you wish to write for. I recommend fifteen minutes to start and only write up until the timer goes off, no longer. If you don't use all fifteen minutes, that's okay, but don't go longer than that. You don't want to be engulfed in shadow work as it can get heavy.

**Step 3:** Write a topic at the top of each page: Shame, anger, worry, guilt, jealousy, resentment. When you are ready, write all you can about these topics, whatever comes up for you. It could be recent events or even things that happened a long time ago. Just keep writing.

**Step 4:** Once you have filled your shadow journal for the decided amount of time, it's now time to release it. Do this ritually, however it feels appropriate. You might wait until the dark moon under the dark of night. Ideally, set up a place to burn the shadow journal outside.

**Step 5:** When you are ready to release, read the entire shadow journal first, everything you've written. Reflect on all that's come up for you.

**Step 6:** When you are ready, rip the pages from the journal and throw them into the fire. Watch as they burn. Notice how you feel, and record any messages or insights you gain from this process in your journal for your own keeping.

## Removing Self-Limiting Beliefs

When you dive into the depths of your shadow and assess what is hidden as well as what is known to you, you may discover or become aware of self-limiting beliefs. These are beliefs that have a negative effect on your potential. Usually, limiting self-beliefs are formed in response to painful experiences, often in our early years. From these experiences, we create our own views of who and how we are in life. These generalizations of life become part of us and are integrated into our subconscious. They commonly show up as beliefs that affect our view of the world and much of what we think.[12] In order to work through these beliefs, we must first recognize them so they may be challenged.

## EXERCISE
### The Four Questions of the Work

One way that has helped me work through limiting beliefs is through a sort of form of self-directed cognitive therapy that Byron Katie has created that she refers to as "The Work."[13] The four questions are:

1. Is it true?
2. Can I absolutely know that it's true?
3. How do I react when I believe that thought?
4. Who would I be without the thought?

After exploring the questions, Katie challenges you to come up with a "turnaround"—a sentence expressing the opposite of that belief.

For example, "I hate myself for being sick so much" could turn into "I may not be well all the time, but I can still love myself no matter my health." This sentence could then be rephrased as "In order for me to be happy, I need to not be sick all the time." Next, we ask the questions again. Is this true? We might answer yes based on the feelings involved with this situation.

Let's dig deeper: "Can I absolutely know that it's true?" The answer there is "not really." You might be happier than when you are sick sometimes, but you might not feel any different.

Next: "How do I react when you believe that thought?" "Likely very bitter, disgruntled, and weighed down. Possibly helpless because I don't have my own power to change the circumstance."

12. Integrity Coaching and Leadership Development, "How to Overcome Self-Limiting Beliefs," accessed August 18, 2023, https://www.integritycoaching.co.uk/blog/overcoming-the-challenges-of-headship/self-limiting-beliefs.
13. Tom Moon, "The Four Liberating Questions," The Work of Byron Katie, accessed September 15, 2023, https://thework.com/2017/10/four-liberating-questions.

Ask the next question, "Who would I be without the thought?" and the answer is likely "I'd feel a lot lighter and happier. I might even feel a bit better physically, as I'm not dwelling on feeling sick."

Now, turn the thought around into its opposite. "I don't hate myself for being sick all the time. I don't need to feel better in order to be happy. Believing I'm unhappy because I am sick is keeping me unhappy." Ultimately, this is a good takeaway. You may tell yourself at the end something like, "I need to admit that I'm hurting myself by ruminating on being sick all the time. Instead of waiting for good days to be happy, maybe I need to focus on feeling happy on bad days too."

## Blessing Your Body

One idea to get in touch with your body and empower yourself is to bless your imperfect body and get to a place where you love your body. The idea for doing my own body blessing came to me while I was writing something for a funeral. Usually, if it is a witch or Pagan death, the officiant will bless the body of the deceased. I have done this before many times but wasn't regularly practicing blessing my own living vessel. And so I set off to write a blessing in a similar vein to my body blessing for the dead. I use this in times when I am frustrated with my body or feel like I need some self-love and care.

### EXERCISE
### Body Blessing Ritual

To do this exercise, gather the items listed but also gather anything else that signifies to you self-love and care. Do this ritual in front of your self altar.

#### You will need

Rose or frankincense incense
Power and Attraction Oil (recipe on page 80)
Bowl of water
Salt
Lighter or matches

Stand before your self altar with all your spell components at the ready. Get yourself into a comfortable state.

### Preparing for Ritual

Check in with all parts of yourself and do a body scan. Then walk through the process of aligning your cauldrons.

Add salt to the bowl of water. Starting in the north, dip your fingers in the salt water and sprinkle it around the circle. Say aloud: *I cleanse this space by earth and water.*

Light the incense and walk around the circle starting in the north, wafting the smoke to cleanse the space. Say aloud: *I cleanse this space by fire and air.*

### Casting the Circle

With the altar in front of you, raise your wand or use your dominant hand. Moving around the circle in a clockwise manner, say aloud:

*I cast this circle to protect us from harm on all levels.*
*I consecrate this circle to allow only the most perfect*
*energies in and to block out all others.*
*I charge this circle to be a space beyond space,*
*a time beyond time, a temple of perfect love and perfect trust.*
*Where only the highest will reigns sovereign.*
*So mote it be!*

### Calling the Quarters

Call the quarters in a clockwise manner. Start by facing north. Raise your left hand and call:

*To the north, I call upon Great Stag and the element of earth. Please guard and guide us in this circle. Hail and welcome.*

Face east. Raise your left hand and call:

*To the east, I call upon Mighty Horse and the element of fire. Please guard and guide us in this circle. Hail and welcome.*

Face south. Raise your left hand and call:

*To the south, we call upon Wise Crow and the element of air. Please guard and guide us in this circle. Hail and welcome.*

Face west. Raise your left hand and call:

*To the west, we call upon Changing Snake and the element of water. Please guard and guide us in this circle. Hail and Welcome.*

## Calling the Guides and Allies and Setting Intention

Facing your altar, state aloud:

*I call upon the Goddess, God, and Great Spirit.*
*I call to my guides and I call to the angels.*
*I call to the Ascended Masters and I call upon the Mighty Dead.*
*I call to the Hidden Company,*
*the witches who have walked this path before me.*
*I invite you to guide and guard me in the space as I do my work.*
*I call upon the ancestors, I call to the beloved dead.*
*I call upon those of my own who are healthy, well, and able in Spirit,*
*Oversee this rite and may it be for my highest healing good,*
*harming none.*
*So mote it be.*

## The Work

Light the incense and waft the smoke over your body, starting at the top of your head and then moving down to your feet. Take the Power and Attraction Oil and anoint yourself with a small amount of oil on each area as you move through each section of the body. Do not apply oil to the eyes or genitals, or to the inside of mouth. State aloud:

## Blessing of the Living Vessel

*I stand in reverence*
*with grounded feet upon the earth,*
*to honor and bless this living vessel bestowed to me.*
*I bless my crown, my intellect,*

*my sovereign and wise head.*
*I bless my brow, and my open eyes,*
*the windows out which I view the world.*
*I bless my ears that listen well.*
*I bless my nose that smells the ocean breeze.*
*I bless my lips that speak my truth.*
*I bless my throat that gives me voice and song.*
*I bless my shoulders that carry myself and others through challenge,*
*and my arms that embrace dear ones.*
*I bless my hands that reach out and shape my destiny,*
*and reach for another's hand.*
*I bless my heart that nurtures myself and others,*
*and for the love I have to share,*
*I bless my chest, my ribs and lungs,*
*that move with my breath as tides rise and fall.*
*I bless my solar plexus, my center,*
*that houses my confidence and will.*
*I bless my belly and insides,*
*nourishing and sustaining my body.*
*I bless my hips and buttocks,*
*that dance, shake, and move.*
*I bless my sex and sacrum,*
*that share pleasures, creation, and delight.*
*I bless my thighs, their support and strength.*
*I bless my knees that march forth with might.*
*I bless the legs that stand on the shoulders of the ancestors,*
*and carry me through life.*
*I bless the feet that walk upon this earth,*
*And send immense gratitude for the miracle I am.*

### Raising the Energy

In a sweeping motion, gather the energy up with your hands. When you've collected it, push the energy up and out of the circle with the extended sounds of "E-A-O" (pronounced "ee-ah-oh").

Then place your hands across your chest to ground the work in yourself or place your hands upon the ground to send some energy back to the earth.

### Release the Guides and Allies

Facing your altar, say aloud:

*I thank and release the Goddess, God, and Great Spirit.*
*I thank and release my guides and the angels,*
*I send thanks to the Ascended Masters and the Mighty Dead.*
*I send thanks to the Hidden Company,*
*the witches who have walked this path before me.*
*I send thanks to the ancestors,*
*and to the beloved dead who gathered here,*
*Thank you for overseeing this rite and may it be*
*for my highest healing good, harming none.*
*So mote it be.*

### Release the Quarters

Release the quarters counterclockwise while raising your right hand. Start in the north and move west. At each cardinal point, say aloud:

*To the north, I thank and release the Great Stag and the element of earth. Thank you for guiding and guarding us in this circle. Hail and farewell.*

*To the west, I thank and release Changing Snake and the element of water. Thank you for guiding and guarding us in this circle. Hail and farewell.*

*To the south, I thank and release Wise Crow and the element of air. Thank you for guiding and guarding us in this circle. Hail and farewell.*

*To the east, I thank and release Mighty Horse and the element of fire. Thank you for guiding and guarding us in this circle. Hail and farewell.*

### Closing the Circle

Moving counterclockwise with your raised wand or dominant hand, say aloud:

> *I cast this circle out into the cosmos as a sign of my work. The circle is open but unbroken. So mote it be!*

## Avoiding Toxic Positivity

Those who've known me a long time remember my "Be Positive" days. In my early twenties, I was heavily influenced by the New Age/New Thought movement. I spent a lot of energy trying to think positively in times when things were not good. It served its purpose and did get me through a lot, but at the same time, I know now it was spiritual bypassing; I was ignoring the larger picture and ultimately delayed my processing of what was really happening or had happened to me.

Spiritual bypassing is a term that describes the use of spiritual explanations to avoid complex psychological issues. At its essence, it is the "tendency to use spiritual ideas and practices to sidestep or avoid facing unresolved emotional issues, psychological wounds, and unfinished developmental tasks."[14] You may have heard or even used phrases such as "Everything happens for a reason" or "It was for the best." The privilege that comes with being able to think positively while not confronting real issues as well as spiritual narcissism goes hand in hand with spiritual bypassing.

As someone involved in the death positivity movement, one of my greatest pet peeves is when after a death someone says "they are in a better place" or that it was "part of God's plan." Other commonly used phrases that chronically ill folks have likely heard are "Good vibes only" and "Thoughts and prayers!" I have a special place in my angst around sending thoughts and prayers. If you are actually going to send prayers and the person has consented to being sent that energy, fine. Otherwise, I don't need

14. Gabriela Picciotto, Jesse Fox, and Félix Neto, "A Phenomenology of Spiritual Bypass: Causes, Consequences, and Implications," *Journal of Spirituality in Mental Health* 20, 2 (2018): 333–354.

your energy being blasted my way, especially if it is coming with other feelings tied to it such as pity or judgmental thoughts or prayers for the salvation of my soul. It's also common for people to say they are going to send them and then don't, so it just becomes an empty phrase without meaning or action. If I say I'm going to send someone healing, I do it. If I can't, I will say something that reflects what can be done at the time. We're a society that acts pleasant but isn't always pleasant.

Honor your feelings when you feel terrible. Process the emotions that come up for you. Fear, anger, depression, anxiety, whatever it is. If you just ignore those feelings by thinking positively, they will eventually fester, which is what I found out by spending years trying to be above it all with my positive outlook on life. Eventually, the work we are avoiding will rear its head, and we'll be forced to face it—and we should. This is another reason why journaling through good and bad days is such an effective process. Using a mantra can also help us here.

## EXERCISE
## Magickal Amu-Let-It-Go

Amulets are charms often used for protection. I think of amulets as charms warding against something or letting it go. They are similar to talismans, though talismans are usually used to bring in or manifest something. Here is a way to enchant an amulet to help release energy that does not serve you when you are having a bad day or when someone says something icky to you.

### You will need

A wearable piece of jewelry. It could already have a protection symbol, such as the evil eye on it or just be a piece of jewelry that you like and wish to use for this purpose. You could consider using jewelry with a stone of protection such as tiger's eye or obsidian.

Smoke to cleanse the jewelry. This could be incense, palo santo, or other sacred herbs.

**Step 1:** Light your media to create sacred smoke. Take your piece of jewelry and pass it through the smoke three times, saying aloud: *I cleanse and clear this jewelry. May it be clear for me to program. So mote it be.*

**Step 2:** Hold the jewelry in your hands. Speak aloud your intentions for the jewelry. You could use *I ask in the name of the Goddess, God, and Great Spirit, under the watchful eyes of the ancestors, that this jewelry be consecrated to banish any unwanted or harmful energy directed at me. I ask that this energy be transmuted into helpful, harmonious energy for my highest healing good. Thank you to all those who aid in this work. So mote it be!*

**Step 3:** Wear your amu-let-it-go as a ward.

## Using Affirmations

Affirmations, or positive affirmations, are short and powerful statements that help overcome negative or unhelpful thought patterns. Creating positive affirmations about ourselves and our abilities can help us overcome self-sabotaging and negative thoughts and instead manifest a positive and confident mindset. Most of us with chronic illness are familiar with challenging mindsets; the stress of managing overall health in a complicated health care system, as well as managing symptoms of a chronic illness, can take a large toll on mental health and wellness. While sometimes it's hard to see the forest for the trees, your illness does *not* define you. Affirmations can help you focus on health and personal improvement while not being dismissive of what you're actually facing day to day. The main goal of doing affirmations is to create a better environment for you to heal and thrive at your own pace.

Here are some examples of chronic illness and health affirmations:

- I am capable of healing and magick.
- My health is improving every day.
- I am grateful for my body and its capabilities.
- I am able to care for my body and all its needs.
- I listen to the wisdom of my body.
- I am peaceful and calm.

- Asking for help is not a weakness.
- I am strong in my body and mind.
- I am growing and learning from my experiences.
- I embrace my healing journey.
- I am worthy.
- I am deserving of rest and relaxation.
- I have compassion for my body and mind.
- My self-worth is not dependent on the approval of others.
- I am confident in my ability to overcome challenges and emerge stronger and wiser.
- I focus on what I can control in my life.

Once you find an affirmation that resonates with you, try to do your affirmations at the same time each day so that they become part of your routine. While affirmations on their own are helpful, pairing affirmations with ritual technology can add power to your affirmations. To lend some oomph to your affirmation practice, you could create a ritual for it or add to an existing one. When you raise the energy, repeat your affirmation and release it into the world. You could also amplify affirmations by using music and movement. Getting into the feel of the affirmation while you are saying it makes it all the more effective. I have done this with much success. The more you feel it, the more effective it will be.

## EXERCISE
### Bad Day Tea

Tea can comfort and support you with its healing properties and partnership with spirit allies. When you are having a bad day, it can be easy to choose to do nothing and forgo the magick. If you are in that kind of funk, here's a tea recipe you can make ahead of time for those moments when you've just had enough. This tea is a tasty, earthy, rooty blend with a little bit of calendula to add sunshine that helps you and your body detox from a bad day (not to mention it supports the liver and kidneys). This tea also helps to cleanse, purify, and get you "rooted" so you can get your groove back.

### You will need

4 tablespoons burdock root
3 tablespoons dandelion root
2 tablespoons nettle leaves
2 tablespoons licorice root
1 tablespoon calendula flowers

Mix together with your hands, thanking each herb for lending its support to this tea. Steep 1 tablespoon with a cup of hot but not boiling water. Makes 12 cups.

## Creating Meditation Beads

One form of meditation that I've found empowering is the use of beads. Beads have been used in spiritual practices across cultures and traditions throughout time. Perhaps the most well-known examples of using beads with prayer are mala beads in Buddhist and Hindu practices as well as Catholic rosaries. Beads can be used in a variety of ways to help meditation. Starting this practice is easy: Holding a strand of beads, let them drape across your fingers so they can move easily. Place two fingers around one of the beads. Take a full breath, inhaling and exhaling once per bead. Repeat with every bead on the strand.

A mantra is a phrase, word, or sound you can use to help focus your awareness during meditation. Most people are familiar with "om," which is an easy one for beginners. "Om" is considered the universal sound. You could also use an affirmation as described in the last section for each bead. I find spoken words to be powerful and mostly use my beads with spoken words. If you cannot speak out loud due to your current situation, you can say it in your head or whisper it. Ultimately, any act of mediation and mindfulness is worth doing.

## EXERCISE
### Affirmations with Meditation Beads

Prayer beads come in all types of material and lengths. I have several sets of stone malas that I work with when I visited India. I chose stones that resonate with my goals and personal constitution. You might consider doing something similar to amplify your practices. There are also sacred woods. Making your own plastic one can be just as effective. Find what calls to you.

### You will need

A string of beads; you might choose stone beads that relate to your goal for meditation

### Optional

Incense or sacred smoke that lends itself to your affirmation's goal

**Step 1:** If you are using it, light the incense. Cleanse yourself and the beads with sacred smoke.

**Step 2:** Get yourself into a comfortable position, ideally with spine straight but make adjustments for your comfort and ability. Take a few centering breaths in and out.

**Step 3:** Hold the string of beads in your dominant hand.

**Step 4:** Touching the first bead or what will be the starting bead on a string of beads, state your affirmation aloud. For example, *I am grateful for my body and its capabilities.*

**Step 5:** Move your fingers to the next sequential bead. Repeat the affirmation: *I am grateful for my body and its capabilities.*

**Step 6:** Do this for a determined number of beads that feels right for you (mine has around a hundred). If your beads are in a circle, do this continuously. If you reach the end of your string, flip it over and start again from the end.

# PART THREE
# Finding Allies

CHAPTER 9
# Healing Spirits

Healing spirits can take on many shapes and forms. If you work within a specific pantheon, it is likely you will find a healing deity to connect with, and you may even already have a relationship. If you are new to working with spirits, this chapter will provide some ideas on how to meet a healing spirit guide and how to explore your own spirit of disease relationship.

## Connecting with a Healing Guide

If you're new to the world of connecting with healing guides, fear not, for it is often a powerful experience that can greatly benefit navigating a chronic illness. The process of meeting a healing guide shares some similarities with connecting to spirits of the dead and spirit guides. Let's begin with some friendly etiquette to help you on your path.

You might wonder, "How will I recognize my healing guide?" Spirits often have unique ways of presenting themselves—they could come in the form of a name, a color, a sound, a vision, or even a comforting feeling. Let go of any preconceived notions about what you should hear, see, sense, or feel, and embrace the diversity of ways in which Spirit can establish its signature. For example, I have one guide who doesn't have a name that I'm aware of but I perceive as my "blue guide." I sense the energy of this guide and see them as a shining blue light. While I prefer spirits with names that are more straightforward, that's not always how they show up. I have connected with this guide for a long time and trust and know their energy and color when it appears, and that's good enough for our relationship. It must have been what I needed at the time I met them. Spirits have a knack for choosing names or appearances that resonate with us, making interactions comfortable and accessible.

When you first encounter a new healing guide, it's a good practice to approach the interaction with openness and curiosity. Begin by observing the interaction and consider asking the spirit how they prefer to be acknowledged. As the spirit draws near, inquire if they have a name and how they would like to be addressed. It's always courteous to respect their preferences, as this paves the way for harmonious connections.

Building a strong bond with your healing guide requires commitment, so it is helpful to integrate this practice into your daily routine or as a significant part of your life. Don't hesitate to request signs and seek assistance from your healing guide. Be receptive to communication, and remember that oftentimes the key to success is simply allowing yourself to be open and attuned to the messages and signs that spirits are sending your way.

Consider setting aside specific moments to connect with your guides at your self altar or at another altar where you make spirit contact. Dedicated time offers opportunities for devotion, receiving messages, and seeking guidance. Embrace this journey with an open heart, and you'll find yourself on a path to healing for your highest good guided by caring spirits who are eager to support you.

## *Healing Deities*

Healing deities are powerful allies for your healing journey. If you already work with deities or are interested in starting a relationship with them, building a devotional practice can be a respectful and powerful place to start. I've listed some healing deities here that you may wish to research further and explore working with.

***Brigid:*** Irish goddess associated with healing

***Sekhmet:*** Egyptian goddess of healing and medicine

***Isis:*** Egyptian goddess of healing, magic, marriage, and protection

*Apollo:* Greek god of medicine, healing and plagues, and prosperity healing

*Asclepius:* Greek god of the medicinal arts

*Chiron:* Greek centaur known for his knowledge and skill in medicinal arts

*Hygieia:* Greek goddess of cleanliness and sanitation

*Panacea:* Greek goddess of healing by medicines and salves

## EXERCISE
## Meeting Your Healing Guide

In this exercise, connect with your healing guide who can support you on your healing journey. Meeting your healing spirit guide can be the start of a lifelong connection for those navigating chronic illness. Our goal here is to create a warm and welcoming space for you to connect with your healing guide, spirit, or deity so that you have a healing experience.

For this and all journey work, always make your environment conducive to the work. Find a peaceful, comfortable, and relaxed physical space where you won't be disturbed. Light a candle, let incense waft through the air, or play soft, soothing music to set a pleasant atmosphere. If you have an altar or meditation space already set up, that will be ideal to conduct this exercise.

You may wish to record this guided experience and play it back for yourself.

### You will need

Incense, such as frankincense or copal

### Optional

A way to play soft music
A way to record and play back the meditation
A journal to record your experience

*Close your eyes, and take a deep breath in, and exhale slowly. Focus on the natural rhythm of your breath, and allow yourself to feel comfortable, calm, and peaceful. You're entering a meditative state where everything you do is for your highest good.*

*Envision the numbers as we count them down: twelve, eleven, ten, nine, eight, seven, six, five, four, three, two, one.*

*Imagine yourself in an empty place, a blank canvas where you can manifest anything you desire. Here, you'll craft a beautiful, safe, and tranquil space to connect with your spirit guides. It's a space that's uniquely yours, known only to you and your guides. Start by creating a comfortable chair or any relaxing spot you prefer. It could be something you already own or perhaps a natural setting, like a riverside stone, the ground beneath a tree, or even a fluffy cloud.*

*Visualize every detail of your chosen spot. If there's a chair, for example, notice its color, textures, and even its scent. See everything vividly in your mind's eye. Now, imagine yourself sitting or lying down, fully relaxed. This is your special place to rest and rejuvenate.*

*Continue to create your special place by adding walls, a floor, and a ceiling, or imagine it in a serene natural setting. Let your imagination run wild—there are no limits here. Personalize this space with flowers, ornaments, or decor that brings you joy, safety, and comfort.*

*Make this special room a part of you, etching every detail into your memory. You can return here whenever you wish, making changes or adjustments as needed. This space is your haven, where you'll always feel safe, comfortable, and relaxed.*

*As you relax in your comfortable space, completely safe and secure, become aware of the presence of a guide just outside your space. Perhaps you hear their footsteps approaching. When you're ready, invite your healing guide into your space by simply thinking about them and asking them to come closer.*

*As your healing guide enters your space, you'll see them clearly. Take in every detail of their face, features, hair, clothes, and physical presence. Observe the joy in their eyes as they greet you, and feel the happiness radiating from both of you. Your perception of them is unique and perfect for this experience.*

*Focus your attention on your healing guide, and let your thoughts flow naturally. Begin by asking any questions you feel are appropriate, such as:*

*What is your name, or by what shall I call you?*

*Why are you an important healing guide for me right now?*

*Do you have a message for me?*

*How may I honor you?*

*When your conversation with your guide is complete, express your gratitude for the wisdom and answers you've received. Watch as your guide prepares to leave, knowing that you can speak to them whenever you desire simply by thinking of them. Escort your healing guide to the edge of your space, offer your thanks, and say goodbye for today. Close the space's boundary, and return to your seat.*

*Take a moment to contemplate the wisdom, advice, and guidance you've received. Commit it to your memory so that you can easily access this information in the future, just by thinking about your experience.*

*Count up from your meditative state: one, two, three, four, five, six, seven, eight, nine, ten, eleven, twelve. Feel your fingers and toes gently stretching. When you're ready, open your eyes.*

Remember to journal your experience, noting any messages or visions received during this meditation. Repeat this exercise as often as you like, allowing your connection with your healing guide to grow stronger with each interaction.

## The Spirits of Disease

Have you ever thought about the concept that your disease or malady has a spirit? This was a fascinating exploration after my blood disorder ordeal. When I sat to mediate and seek answers about my illness, I started to encounter the spirits of my dis-eases. There, I used it. I know a lot of healing modalities discuss the term "dis-ease," where whatever ailment you might have has a source rooted in your life causing lack or dis-ease. And to a degree, I believe there are some corresponding attributes, but certainly not to the level that it's possible to have summoned or caused your disease. We'll discuss this idea more later, but my point here is that diseases have spirits, and just like working with any spirit, you can connect and interface with these beings.

Quite a few years back, I recall seeing some art that depicted mental health conditions in monster form. Artist Toby Allen created a series called *Real Monsters* that he says is an ongoing personal project exploring mental health through character design.[15] The project aims to reduce the stigma surrounding mental illness and educate about less well-known conditions.

In his work, the monsters have short stories about how they interact with the world and what they have domain over, which corresponds to the symptoms of the illness they represent. This art project fascinated me, so I started exploring it more. Those explorations have led to revelations about why I may be experiencing what I do in this lifetime. Again, I don't believe I did anything to "deserve" getting sick, but there can be connections made in your ancestral lineage or possibly past lives. If this idea doesn't resonate with you, perhaps that is not where your connection lies. From connecting with the spirit of TTP, my blood disorder, I feel a connection to primordial ancestors—not anyone I would recognize, something that goes further back. I feel this connection from the way the spirit presented itself to me and the messages I've received around it. Out of all my illnesses and afflictions, this one has been the most tricky to connect to in a way I am familiar with, probably because it is so primordial. It lacks a persona that some of the other spirits I've connected to have.

The spirit of arthritis, for example, appears to me as an old woman who looks twisted and pained. Now, is this the true form of the spirit? It doesn't matter to me, as it is how we communicate. If you connect with the spirit of arthritis, you may see something completely different, and that is okay.

If you have experience with spirit work, a lot of the same techniques that you are probably familiar with can work for connecting to your spirits of disease. If you are new, I've included a meditation to make contact with a spirit of disease as a jumping-off point if this is something you wish to explore.

15. Toby Allen, "Real Monsters," Zesty Does Things, accessed August 20, 2023, https://www.zestydoesthings.com/realmonsters.

## EXERCISE
### Spirit House for Spirits of Disease

I have found that giving my spirits of disease a spirit house in the form of a clay doll can give them an anchoring point to connect with where the spirits may freely come and go. I did not craft this doll in my image but as a body for spirits to inhabit while they makes contact. I keep this doll in a box on my self altar and only take it out when I am setting the intention of connecting with a spirit of disease. This is just my process; it isn't based on any lore or tradition known to me. I don't mind connecting with these spirits at my self altar because these spirits are part of my life and dwell within me too.

#### You will need

Enough clay to create a doll the size of your liking (mine is about the size of my hand)
Loose frankincense resin
Small quartz crystal
Small amount of wormwood
Spoon or clay tools

**Step 1:** Craft a doll form out of clay. This doll is not intended to be in your likeness; it is a generic body form. I've chosen to make mine androgynous.

**Step 2:** Hollow out the back of the clay doll with a tool or spoon. Make the hole big enough to place your items in, but not so deep that it carves through to the front of the doll.

**Step 3:** Hold the frankincense in your hands and say aloud, *Frankincense, I ask that you lend me your powers so that my spirit work with this doll can be amplified. Thank you for your blessings.* Place the frankincense in the hollowed space in the doll.

**Step 4:** Hold the quartz crystal in your hands and say aloud, *Quartz, I ask that you lend me your powers so that my spirit work with this doll can be amplified. Thank you for your blessings.* Place the quartz crystal into the hollowed space in the doll.

**Step 5:** Hold the wormwood in your hands and say aloud, *Wormwood, I ask that you lend me your powers so that my spirit work with this doll can be amplified. Thank you for your blessings.* Place the wormwood into the hollowed space in the doll.

**Step 6:** Using more clay, seal the opening on the back of the doll shut.

**Step 7:** Lay the doll flat before you (at your self altar is a good location). With your two pointer fingers touching each other and your two thumbs also touching each other, form a triangle shape with your hands. Hover your hands in this position over the doll and say, *I enliven this doll as a working spirit house. May the spirits I call forth have a safe anchoring space for the purpose of communion. May there only be peace between us.* If you would like to add stipulations or guidelines to working with particular spirits of disease, you can add them here.

**Step 8:** Blow your breath in the triangle formed with your hands three times onto the doll.

**Step 9:** Say aloud, *So mote it be!*

**Step 10:** Your doll is now ready to be worked with and you can use it to call forth the spirits of disease you wish to commune with.

## Commune with the Spirit of Your Disease

Once you have set out to connect with the spirit of your disease, what's next? Here's a list of some questions or intentions that can be explored with your spirit. Choose a few that you would like to ask your spirit before you start the following exercise.

- What is your name?
- What may I call you?
- What do you look like?
- Is there a purpose for you to be with me?
- Is there something I need to know from you?
- What can I do to bring ease to living with you?

- Where do you come from?
- Do we have any ancestral ties?
- If so, are there specific ancestors with whom you are connected?
- Do we have any past life or karmic ties?
- If so, is there anything I can do to help remedy some of the issues?
- Are you here temporarily, or will you be with me throughout my life?
- Is there anything I can do to help you to not interfere with my daily life?
- Do you have any messages for me at this time?
- Am I connecting with the correct health providers to work with you at this time?
- Am I on the correct medications to help ease or eliminate your symptoms?
- Is there anything more I can be doing to help myself with your afflictions?

Sometimes you may get a response, sometimes you may not. I find that some spirits are more interactive and personal, whereas some are aloof, amorphous, or more generalized than personal. I find that sometimes I am connecting with *my* spirit of the disease versus sometimes connecting to the overall spirit of the disease. This can feel quite different.

As with any spirit work, brushing up on your psychic and mediumship skills will help. You don't necessarily have to connect with your specific disease—you could connect to a particular malady or ailment that comes with your illness. Some ideas on what spirits you might explore connecting with include the spirit of:

- Chronic fatigue
- Migraines
- Anxiety
- PTSD
- Your autoimmune disease

- Arthritis
- ADHD
- Depression
- Social anxiety
- Nightmares

## EXERCISE
### Communing with the Spirit of Your Disease

As with the other journeys, find a quiet, peaceful space where you won't be disturbed. You may want to record this narration and play it back to have a guided experience. During the journey, consider visiting the space created in the Meeting Your Healing Guide exercise (page 127) as a starting point to invite your spirit of disease to connect with you. Or you may wish to meet in a different location as used in what follows. Either will work; it is simply a matter of preference.

#### You will need

Incense such as frankincense or copal

#### Optional

A way to play soft music
A way to record and play back the meditation
A journal to record your experience

#### Begin Your Journey

*Sit or lie down in a comfortable position, ensuring you're relaxed and at ease. Take a few deep breaths to center yourself. Close your eyes, and take a moment to set your intention. Acknowledge that you're here to connect with the spirit of your disease, seeking insight and wisdom. Let go of any preconceived notions and approach this with an open heart and mind.*

*Envision the numbers as we count them down: twelve, eleven, ten, nine, eight, seven, six, five, four, three, two, one.*

*You find yourself in a serene and safe environment around you. Feel the energy of this place enveloping you, providing comfort and protection.*

*Ask the spirit of your disease to come forward and connect with you. Visualize the presence of the spirit of your disease. You may see it in a form that's personal to you, or it may appear differently than you would expect. This spirit may look humanoid or take an unfamiliar shape. Extend an invitation to this spirit, welcoming it into your meditative space. Ask the spirit to join you with the intention of understanding its purpose and how you may partner together for healing.*

*As you meet with your spirit of disease, greet it with respect and openness. Begin by asking questions you are seeking answers to, allowing time for answers or insights to arise.*

*After each question, take a moment to listen and observe. Pay attention to any thoughts, feelings, images, or sensations that arise during your meditation. Trust your intuition and allow the spirit to communicate with you in its unique way.*

*When you feel your connection with the spirit of your disease has come to a natural conclusion, express gratitude for the insights and wisdom gained during this journey. Thank the spirit for its presence and understanding.*

*Slowly return your awareness to your physical surroundings. Take a few deep breaths and gently open your eyes. Reflect on your experience and consider journaling your insights for future reference.*

*Return now to the present. Counting up from your meditative state: one, two, three, four, five, six, seven, eight, nine, ten, eleven, twelve. Feel your fingers and toes gently stretching. When you're ready, open your eyes.*

Remember that this meditation is a starting point for your exploration. Your connection with the spirit of your disease may evolve over time, providing you with valuable insights and a deeper sense of self-awareness. Approach this process with patience and openness, knowing that you can always repeat this exercise to gain more clarity on the messages you received.

## Spirits of Medications

In this book I go in-depth about connecting to the spirits of plants in your magickal practice to gain valuable allies for your healing and witchcraft endeavors. Something that has struck me to do in my practice, which admittedly took a while to get on board with, is communing with the spirits of medication. At first when I was put on a long list of medications, I was pretty disappointed. I was sad to stop taking my herbs medicinally and almost felt like it was a failure on my part that I couldn't just "heal" myself. I am a witch, after all. That's how strong my internalized ableism voice gets at times. Alas, after a while and adjusting medications not just for physical ailments but ones that help with anxiety, depression, and overall mental health, I realized how much my medicines help me function. Instead of resenting them, I started to be grateful for taking them and having the ability to access them.

At this turning point, I realize that, much like plant allies, these medications have a constitution as well and a spirit with whom I can connect. I think of it sort of like a servitor, an artificially crafted spirit tasked with a specific job. I once had a servitor that I honestly loved dearly, as it protected the studio space where I worked. I called him Stoodguard, and he patrolled the inside of the studio hallways, protected the physical building, and took care of anything ooky being directed the studio's way. I always thought that it was neat when students in my psychic and mediumship development classes described what he looked like and could feel his presence.

Much like how I experienced Stoodguard, I connect with the spirits of each medication. Some of the names of the medication even sound like spirit names to me. When I make these connections, I ask how we may best partner together and if there is anything I need to know or should do to make our partnership work better. Interestingly, I have received information telling me to avoid certain foods. When I reflected on this more, I realized that one side effect was weight gain, and I think the spirit was trying to guide me to not have that happen. See what shows up for you.

## EXERCISE
### Connecting with the Spirit of Medication

Use this exercise to connect with the spirit of your medications. You might try calling upon one of the names of your medications in similar fashion to the spirit guide meditations to see what you perceive and what answers and information show up from making this connection.

#### You will need

The container of the medication that you wish to make a connection with

**Step 1:** Hold the container of the medication whose spirit you wish to connect with. Get yourself into a comfortable position. Take a few deep breaths to center yourself. Count down the numbers into a meditative state: twelve, eleven, ten, nine, eight, seven, six, five, four, three, two, one.

**Step 2:** Close your eyes, and take a moment to set your intention. Acknowledge that you're here to connect with the spirit of your medication.

**Step 3:** Ask the spirit of your medication to come forward and connect with you. How does the spirit present itself? You may see, feel, hear, or just know something about the spirit. Notice anything you are experiencing.

**Step 4:** Ask the spirit of medication if there is a message for you.

**Step 5:** If you feel guided to, ask how you may reduce any side effects from the medication. Are there things you could do or avoid to help the medication do its job well?

**Step 6:** Express gratitude for the information you've been given. Thank the spirit for its presence and understanding.

**Step 7:** Slowly return your awareness to your physical surroundings. Take a few deep breaths, and gently open your eyes. Reflect on your experience and consider journaling your insights for future reference.

**Step 8:** Return now to the present. Count up from your meditative state: one, two, three, four, five, six, seven, eight, nine, ten, eleven, twelve. Feel your fingers and toes gently stretching. When you're ready, open your eyes.

CHAPTER 10

# Plant Spirit Allies for Chronic Illness

Plant spirit allies are spirit guides from the green world. They can be powerful allies that help with healing but also coping with the reality of chronic illness. The first way to make a connection to a plant spirit ally is to examine what plants you feel called to. What you are drawn to and naturally have an affinity for may be a strong ally for you. I'd also recommend exploring any plants or herbs that you feel a strong aversion to, as there may be lessons from this plant to work through.

## Connecting with Plant Spirit Allies

Plant spirit ally relationships are personal, and while there are common threads woven together from collective experiences, it's possible the plant may communicate or work with you in a way that is nontraditional. Talk out loud to plants. It may seem strange, but bringing forth sound, vibration, and word has tremendous power. When I call to my plant spirit allies in magickal work, I call to them by name. I greet them, thank them, and invite them to do the work or even just to commune and be with me. Experiment with this; the effect is palpable. Other than the highly recommended meditation and journey work, another helpful way of connecting with plant allies is to dream with the plants, especially helpful for healing plant allies. When I am getting to know a new plant and have access to it,

I will take the plant and hang it over my head as I sleep. You could put a small sprig of your plant under your pillow as well or leave it by the side of your bed. Before going to sleep, I will invite the plant to dream with me. Sometimes the dreams are straightforward, and I'm able to meet the plant spirit. What's more likely is that the plant will show me something in a dream for me to work on in partnership with it.

## EXERCISE
## Communing with a Healing Plant Ally

Do this exercise in a quiet, comfortable space. If you have the option, do this exercise outside in nature. You may also prefer to record this exercise and play back the instructions so you can follow along with this meditation. And finally, it's best to write down your experiences in a journal to keep track of how you perceive and connect with your healing plant allies.

### You will need

Incense such as frankincense or copal

### Optional

A way to play soft music
A way to record and play back the meditation
A journal to record your experience

*Light the incense. Sit or lie down in a comfortable position, ensuring you're relaxed and at ease. Take a couple of deep breaths, inhaling and exhaling. Feel yourself grow roots that grow down deep to the core of Mother Earth. State your intention out loud: "I seek to commune with the spirits of green and meet with the most perfect healing plant ally for my highest good at this time."*

*You are now entering into a meditative state where all you do is for your highest good. Envision the numbers as we count them down. Twelve, eleven, ten, nine, eight, seven, six, five, four, three, two…*

*One. See before you a crooked path leading into a sacred forest. As you enter the woods, you touch a guardian tree and announce yourself and your intentions for this special visit. Call from your heart and proclaim that you enter these woods as a friend, a witch, or however you spiritually identify. You call out that you seek to commune with the spirits of green and meet a healing plant ally for your highest healing good. You walk forward along this path and feel your feet upon the cool earth and a light breeze on your skin. You feel the gentle brush of flora as the plants reach out and graze you as you pass.*

*Notice the sound of these woods: the chirping of birds, the babbling of flowing water, rustling leaves, trees creaking, whispering in the wind. You feel connected to this sacred land and all its spirits of the green realm.*

*Ahead of you on this path, you see a grove with a comfortable space for you to sit and commune with a healing plant ally. As you take a seat, you call to the healing plant ally that is just right for you at this time and seek its counsel. This may be a plant that is familiar to you, or perhaps it is unknown.*

*Whatever shows up for you is most perfect for this experience. Commune with your healing plant ally and receive any wisdom or guidance it may share with you. Ask how you may partner with this plant in your healing or magickal practice. Is there healing offered to you from this plant? What is the medicine and magick it shares with you?*

*With gratitude, thank this plant ally for its healing, wisdom, and connection. You send a final blessing and receive any energy that it may return to you. You stand and leave the grove and make your way back down the path until you leave the woods, knowing you can return whenever you choose. You bid thanks and farewell to the flora and spirits of this place and to your healing plant ally.*

*Count up from your meditative state: one, two, three, four, five, six, seven, eight, nine, ten, eleven, twelve. Feel your fingers and toes gently stretching. When you are ready, you may open your eyes.*

Journal or write down the experiences, messages, or visions shared with you in this meditation. Know you can always repeat this exercise to commune with the spirit of your healing plant ally. Notice each time if your perception of it shifts or changes.

## Plant Allies for Chronic Illness

To work with healing plant allies for your health and well-being, seek a healing plant ally that wishes to partner with you in your practice. Most plants have medicinal and healing properties, so exploring which plants show up for you can have significance. I've included a list of some of my favorite plants to work with and their typical uses.

### *Angelica* (Angelica archangelica)

Magickally, angelica root is excellent for protection, especially for women and children. It is used in purification rituals and for luck and gambling charms. It goes by other names, such as garden angelica, masterwort, and holy ghost. Angelica prefers damp meadows, swampy woods, and slightly acidic soils in cooler climates. Medicinally, angelica roots, seeds, leaves, and stems are all valuable. Angelica is a versatile herb, with properties including astringent, antimicrobial, anti-inflammatory, expectorant, carminative, diuretic, emmenagogue, antispasmodic, and stimulant. It predominantly influences the digestive, urinary, respiratory, and reproductive systems. Angelica resonates with both the Sun and Venus, aligns with Leo, and embodies the fire element with a feminine essence.

### *Ashwagandha* (Withania somnifera)

Magicakally, ashwagandha holds a mythical reputation as an herb of longevity and vitality. It strengthens vital energy, helps us cope with stress, and enhances mental abilities. It is also associated with practices like tantra and sex magic. It's known as ashwagandha, winter cherry, and Indian ginseng. Ashwagandha thrives in dry soil, and its roots are mainly used in medicine and magick. Medicinally, ashwagandha dons multiple hats, serving as an adaptogen, sedative, tonic, immunomodulant, anti-inflammatory, antioxidant, nervine, and antispasmodic. Ashwagandha primarily supports the nervous, immune, and endocrine systems. It can calm and alleviate anxiety and stress. It is beneficial for those with insomnia, as well as enhancing mental powers and memory. It can be useful to enhance physical strength, which can offer support for those debilitated by chronic illness. Ashwagandha aligns with both Venus and Mars and corresponds to Scorpio and Taurus. It embodies the earth element with a masculine essence.

### *Burdock* (Arctium lappa)

Magickally, burdock root is employed to ward off negativity, offer protection, and promote healing. Its deep taproot is associated with grounding properties. Burdock thrives in full sun to partial shade, preferring nutrient-rich soils found in fields, forest edges, and near compost piles.

Burdock improves digestion, acting as a mild bitter and stimulating bile secretion. It enhances lymphatic flow, aiding detoxification. Burdock contributes to healthy skin by addressing internal imbalances. Traditionally, it has a history of use for conditions like gout, kidney stones, rheumatism, and eczema. Its influence spreads across the digestive, integumentary, and nervous systems. Burdock resonates with Venus and has astrological ties to Scorpio. It embodies the water element with a feminine essence.

### *Catnip* (Nepeta cataria)

Magicaklly, catnip is renowned for love, beauty, and happiness spells. It's often used in sachets alongside rose petals to attract love and positive energies. It can also be employed to attract a lusty lover. Catnip is found basking in full sunlight in gardens. The leaves and flowers hold magickal and medicinal properties. Catnip is cherished for its calming effects. It also eases colic, expels gas, and soothes teething discomfort. Catnip offers relief for skin irritations and mild respiratory concerns. Catnip is an antispasmodic herb and is used to help manage cramping. It primarily influences the digestive, nervous, and reproductive systems. Catnip resonates with both Venus and the Moon, aligns with Cancer and embodies the water element with a feminine essence.

### *Elder* (Sambucus nigra)

Magicaklly, elder is a potent tool for banishment, exorcism, and healing. It wards against negativity, protects against misfortune, and repels evil spirits. Planting an elder in your garden safeguards your property from harm. Elder thrives in woodlands, scrub, hedgerows, and on wasteland. Both the delicate flowers and vibrant berries are used in medicine and magick. It primarily lends its support to the immune and respiratory systems. It is considered an immune guardian, and elderberry tinctures or syrups are herbalists' trusty companions at the onset of cold or flu. They reduce the duration of illness by inhibiting virus replication and reinforcing cell walls against viral entry. Elderflower and elderberry are allies during colds, flu, and respiratory infections. As a hot tea, elderflowers stimulate circulation, promote sweating, and aid in detoxification. Elder finds its planetary resonance with Venus and aligns astrologically with Scorpio. It embodies the element of water with a feminine essence.

A note on safety: While elderberry is considered safe when used appropriately, certain parts of the elder plant—namely, the bark, leaves, roots, seeds, and unripe berries—contain alkaloids and cyanogenic glycosides, which should be avoided. Cooking or drying elderberries is the safest route.

### *Hawthorn* (Crataegus spp.)

Magickally, hawthorn is revered for protection and connection with the Fae. Planting it as a hedge around your home wards off unfriendly spirits and protects against malevolent magic. Hawthorn thrives in hardy soil under the full sun's embrace. Hawthorn is an ally of the heart and supports heart health, blood pressure regulation, and improved circulation. Hawthorn's planetary ties include Jupiter and the Sun, and it aligns with Leo and Taurus. It is associated with the element of fire and has a masculine essence.

### *Holy Basil* (Ocimum sanctum)

Commonly known as holy basil, tulsi, and tulasi, holy basil's magic extends to love, exorcism, wealth, flying, and protection. It embodies harmony, happiness, purity, serenity, luck, and good health. The leaves and flowering tops are treasured. It is considered an immune guardian that stimulates the immune system, reduces mucus, and warms the body. It's a go-to ally during times of cool, damp sickness. It primarily supports the nervous, reproductive, respiratory, and digestive systems. Holy basil has correspondence with Jupiter and aligns with Sagittarius. It embodies the element of fire and has a feminine essence.

### *Horsetail* (Equisetum arvense)

Magicaklly, horsetail is a symbol of fertility, snakes, longevity, and cleansing. It strengthens resolve, sets boundaries, and cleanses emotional debris. Horsetail is commonly found near marshes, streams, and rivers. Horsetail is renowned for its effectiveness in addressing fluid retention or edema, kidney and bladder stones, urinary tract infections, incontinence, and kidney/bladder disturbances. It can also aid in cases of arthritis, wounds, and hemorrhoids.

It primarily benefits the digestive system, urinary system, and integumentary system (skin). Horsetail resonates with Saturn, aligns with Capricorn, and embodies the earth element with a feminine essence.

### *Hyssop* (Hyssopus officinalis)

Magicaklly, hyssop is a great ally that is used in purification, protection, cleansing, banishing negative energy, and washing away sin. Hyssop thrives in well-drained soil under full or partial sun. Hyssop is a true friend when it comes to respiratory ailments like colds, the flu, and bronchitis thanks to its expectorant, diaphoretic, and antispasmodic properties. It's also antibacterial, antiviral, and beneficial for intestinal viruses. It lends its support to the respiratory, digestive, immune, and endocrine systems. Hyssop aligns with Jupiter, corresponds to Sagittarius, and embraces the element of fire with a masculine essence.

### *Lavender* (Lavandula spp.)

Lavender's magick promotes peace, cleansing, reconciliation, sharpening the mind, encouraging pure love, and fostering fertility. Lavender thrives in well-drained soil under full sun. Lavender excels as a nervine tonic, soothing anxiety, depression, insomnia, and headaches. Its aroma and use in teas have a calming effect on an anxious mind that brings perspective and clarity. Its healing properties primarily support the digestive, nervous, and circulatory systems. Lavender resonates with Mercury, corresponds to Virgo, and embodies the air element with a feminine essence.

### *Lemon Balm* (Melissa officinalis)

Lemon balm's magickal repertoire includes love potions, aphrodisiacs, fertility spells, and an ability to soothe emotional pains after the end of a relationship. Lemon balm is incredibly adaptable, thriving in nearly any soil and spreading with ease. This delightful herb is also called melissa, balm mint, balm, and sweet balm. Lemon balm is the herbal superstar for alleviating stress, anxiety, and depression. Its ability to uplift and calm makes it a go-to remedy, especially when combined with other calming herbs such as valerian and hops. It's a mood-lifter that gladdens the heart and repairs the nervous system. It aids the digestive, nervous, and immune systems. Lemon balm resonates with the Moon and Neptune and aligns with Pisces. It embodies the element of water and has a feminine essence.

### *Motherwort* (Leonurus cardiaca)

Magickally, motherwort inspires inner trust and confidence, wards off negative forces, and connects to immortality and spiritual healing. It's a protective herb that guards pregnant women and their unborn children. Motherwort thrives in sunny areas, basking in the sun's embrace. Motherwort has a special bond with women throughout their life journeys. It acts as a tonic for menstrual and menopausal symptoms, and it soothes cramps, hormonal imbalances, and emotional fluctuations. During childbirth, it stimulates uterine contractions and calms accompanying anxiety. In the postpartum phase, it eases cramping and offers solace for postpartum depression and anxiety. As a menopausal ally, it moderates hormone levels, providing relief from hot flashes, night sweats, insomnia, mood swings, and depression. It primarily aids the circulatory and reproductive systems. Motherwort's planetary connections are Venus and the Moon, and it harmonizes with Leo and Cancer. It aligns with the element of water and has a feminine essence.

### *Mugwort* (Artemisia vulgaris)

Mugwort's magickal folklore is rich, and it has long been known as an aid to divination and psychic abilities. Often used in dream pillows, it offers protection against disease, bad luck, evil spirits, and possession. Mugwort's presence is ubiquitous—it's found everywhere, often alongside roads and in overgrown lots. Mugwort shines as an emmenagogue, boosting pelvic blood flow and menstruation. Its bitter profile aids digestion and contributes to its mild nervine action, making it suitable for alleviating depression and anxiety. It's also known for its effectiveness against worm infestations, vomiting, convulsions, and promoting circulation. Its main influence is on the reproductive, digestive, and nervous systems. Mugwort's planetary companions are Venus and the Moon, and it harmonizes with Taurus, Cancer, and the element of water. It embodies a feminine essence.

### *Nettle* (Urtica dioica)

Magickally, nettle can be used for protection, enhancing strength and concentration, and nourishing the body, mind, and spirit. It can assist in connecting to the Fae. Burn nettle to banish negativity and unwanted spirits. It can also be included in protection bags or in spells to break curses.

Stinging nettle thrives in full sun to partial shade, favoring nutrient-rich soils in fields, on forest edges, and near compost piles. It also goes by the names nettle leaf and devil's claw. Nettle is a powerful ally in battling allergy symptoms, particularly for hay fever, thanks to its inflammation-reducing compounds. It also proves helpful for arthritis, skin irritations, muscle pain, and kidney stones. It aids the cardiovascular, respiratory, and digestive systems. Nettle's planetary connection is Mars, and it resonates with Scorpio and Aries. Its element is fire, and it has a masculine essence.

### *Rosemary* (Salvia rosmarinus)

Work with rosemary in your magick for matters of fidelity, remembrance, dispelling jealousy, and infusing your workings with potent energy. Rosemary thrives in well-drained soil enriched with organic matter under full sun. Rosemary is universally recognized, with a few poetic aliases such as "dew of the sea" and "Mary's mantle." Rosemary shines in matters concerning the head, stomach, and heart. It makes a superb tonic for memory that enhances mental function and acuity by increasing blood flow and stimulation to the brain. These stimulating actions also help alleviate anxiety, depression, insomnia, lethargy, nervousness, fatigue, exhaustion, stress, headaches, and migraines. In matters of the heart, rosemary acts as a restorative and stimulating cardiotonic. Its nervine effects extend to the heart, relaxing and uplifting the spirit, bringing joy and restoring the nervous system. Rosemary extends its influence to the digestive, nervous, immune, and circulatory systems. Its planetary correspondences are the Sun and the Moon, and Leo is its ruling sign. It represents the element of fire and has a feminine essence.

### *Self-Heal* (Prunella vulgaris)

Magickally, self-heal plays a role in home purification, hunting magick, and gentle protection. It is associated with enhancing physical health and cleansing for those who are unwell. Self-heal thrives in moist woodland soils and waste areas and is characterized by its low-lying, creeping growth; simple leaves; and square stem. It goes by various names, including heal-all, all-heal, and many more. Self-heal has been used traditionally in Western herbal medicine for a range of conditions, including inflammation of the mouth and throat, mouth and throat ulcers, herpes, and sore throats. It showcases antiviral and antibacterial properties, making it a versatile ally against conditions like HIV, herpes, influenza, and bacterial infections. Self-heal is also renowned for its efficacy in managing gastrointestinal inflammation and issues like inflammatory bowel disease, colic, diarrhea, gastroenteritis, dyspepsia, and hemorrhoids. Self-heal benefits the digestive and oral systems. Self-heal's corresponding planet is Venus, and Pisces is its astrological ruler. Its element is water, and it has a feminine essence.

## Flower Essences

One of the most powerful and beneficial ways I have continued to work with herbs is with flower essences. Flower essences are a vibrational remedy made with the energy of flowers that work on the recipient's subtle emotional bodies. Flower essences can work wonders for folks with chronic illness and chronic pain. Using one type of flower essence or a combination can help you address and process the complex feelings often prompted by a diagnosis, flare-up, or challenges related to chronic illness. The most popular flower essences on the market, Bach Flower Remedies Rescue Remedies, are easily accessible and include flower essences of Impatiens, Star of Bethlehem, Cherry Plum, Rock Rose, and Clematis. This combination of essences helps lower stress, grounds a person back in the body in a safe way, and aids with trauma and shock, fears (especially around loss of control), panic, or terror.

Here's a list of some common flower essences along with common ailments they are used to treat. Some of these flower essences may be available for purchase at local health-food stores or from a local herbalist.

***Aspen:*** Soothes fear of the unknown or unknown outcomes

***Beech:*** Calms nerves, quells anger, and lessens intolerance

***Borage:*** Boosts courage and reclaims joy

***Comfrey:*** Aids in releasing the past

***Elm:*** Aids when you are feeling overwhelmed

***Gentian:*** Helps when you've had a setback

***Gorse:*** Encouragement against hopelessness and wanting to give up

***Heartsease:*** Comforts and strengthens the heart and encourages opening up again after loss

***Holly:*** Helps when feeling victimized, supports getting out of funks

***Hyssop:*** Dispels guilt and encourages release, aids in cleansing

***Linden:*** Removes obstacles regarding matters of the heart

***Mustard:*** Helps dispel depression and feelings of gloom

***Pine:*** Helps with guilt and self-blame

***St. John's wort:*** Lets the light into times of darkness

***Self-heal (All Heal):*** Promotes self-healing

***Sunflower:*** Allows us to embody joy again

***Vervain:*** Helps with perfectionism and realizing limitations

***Walnut:*** Helps adapt to change

***Wild oat:*** Aids in times of uncertainty

***Willow:*** Helps with resentment and self-pity

Next are directions to craft your own flower essences. You can also purchase flower essences from someone who respectfully works with the plant world. You can commonly find flower essences for sale at natural food markets, metaphysical stores, and herbalist centers.

## EXERCISE
### Making a Flower Essence

This exercise may be familiar if you've read *Magickal Mediumship,* but I believe it is worth sharing here for the benefits it can provide chronically ill folx. Flower essences are made by allowing the flower or other part of the plant to float on purified water under the sun. The sun imbues the energetic imprint of the flower into the water. There are no herbal or chemical components in a flower essence, only the vibrational essence. These instructions create the mother essence bottle for your flower essence.

The mother essence is used to create the stock and dosage bottles. Stock bottles are traditionally what you purchase when you buy flower essences. These can be diluted to dosage bottles and will go a long way with usage. The dilution increases the effect on the subtle energy levels, which is why it is best to take only a dose level of flower essences—in this case, less is more. Standard doses are typically three drops three times a day, but you can also use a pendulum or muscle test to determine dosage. If you wish to avoid using alcohol as a preservative, you can use glycerin-based essences or essences preserved with apple cider vinegar. These flower essences have the same healing ability but a much shorter shelf life.

Flower essences can be used alone or as a compound with other flower essences or vibrational essences. Look more into the significance of subtle energy work with deeper meanings of flower essences.

### You will need

A small- to medium-sized uncovered glass or crystal bowl

Purified water—you can use distilled or spring water. You will need at least enough to fill 75 percent of your dropper bottle. You also want to have enough water so that the flowers can float on the surface.

Fresh flower or plant for the essence, preferably picked before the dew has dried. Note that only a small amount of the plant is needed; one flower is fine for this purpose.

Brandy (or glycerin or apple cider vinegar)

Dropper bottles and labels

A sunny space where you can set your bowl for at least three hours

**Step 1:** Gather all your materials and make sure they are clean.

**Step 2:** Ask to connect with the plant spirit ally of your flower essence. Speak from your heart. Ask for permission to create the flower essence and to take a flower or portion of the plant. If you receive permission, continue to step 3.

**Step 3:** Harvest the flower or portion of the plant you will be using for the flower essence. If you have a ceremonial blade such as a boline or herb scythe, use it here. Thank the plant for its sacrifice.

**Step 4:** Pour the purified water into the glass or crystal bowl.

**Step 5:** Place the bowl of water in the sunny space.

**Step 6:** Float the flower or plant part on the water's surface.

**Step 7:** Let the sun and its energies help transfer the plant's vibrational energies to the water. Leave the bowl in direct sunlight for at least three hours.

**Step 8:** Thank the spirit of the plant and leave the flower out in nature or place it on an altar.

**Step 9:** Fill 75 percent of your dropper bottle with the water, making sure there are no plant parts included.

**Step 10:** Fill the remaining 25 percent of the bottle with brandy to act as a preservative. If you are using glycerin or apple cider vinegar, add it now.

**Step 11:** Label the dropper bottle with the name of the plant, the strength of the essence (mother, stock, or dosage), what is in the bottle, the date it was created, and the location where it was gathered. For example:

Comfrey Flower Essence
Mother Essence Bottle
Preserved in Brandy
August 2024
Crossroads Farm, NH

**Step 12:** If you choose, create stock and dosage bottles.

## To Create a Stock Bottle

**Step 1:** Fill a dropper bottle with 75 percent water and 25 percent brandy (or glycerin/cider).

**Step 2:** Add seven drops from the mother essence bottle.

**Step 3:** Label the bottle with appropriate information.

## To Create a Dosage Bottle

**Step 1:** Fill a dropper bottle with 75 percent water and 25 percent brandy (or glycerin/cider).

**Step 2:** Add seven drops from the stock essence bottle.

**Step 3:** Label the bottle with appropriate information.

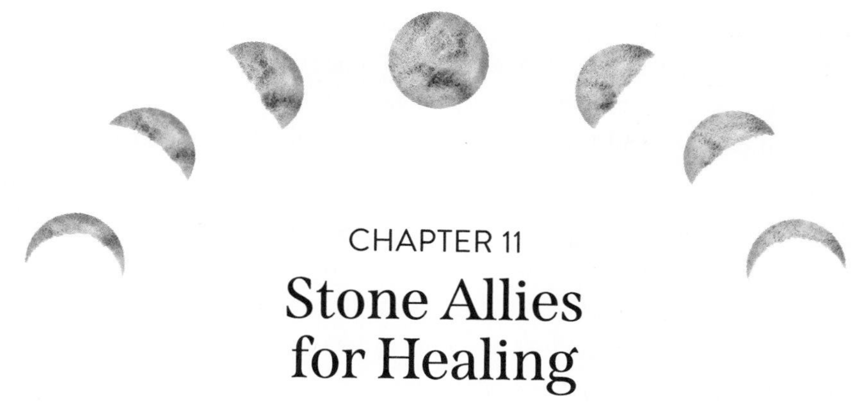

CHAPTER 11

# Stone Allies for Healing

In addition to working with the spirits of plants, I also very much enjoy working with the spirits of crystals and stones. In this section, we'll explore ways to work with the mineral world. My practice has been deepened by respectfully working with spirits of stones, animals, and plants. They can magickally enhance and aid your physical, mental, emotional, and spiritual well-being, which will in turn be beneficial for much of what chronic illness throws at you!

## Stone Spirit Allies

Stones are great spirit allies to partner with for healing purposes and enhancing your mental well-being. These are both beneficial when you are living with an ongoing illness. Working with crystals continues to be one of the most popular ways to connect and energetically work with healing and to connect to spirit allies. If you are new to working with stones, working with crystals is a perfect jumping-off point to becoming more acquainted with how energy feels.

Each stone has its own vibration and frequency and can be a conduit for energy. Stone energies have been used since ancient times for physical healing, emotional well-being, mentality enhancement, and spiritual amplification and as sacred tools of connection to the Divine and the spirit world. Stones are easy to intuit, as the colors, shapes, and textures are significant and contribute to the energy the stones produce. Even someone with minimal stone knowledge can make a connection and receive benefits based purely on the energy produced from the visual aesthetic or tactile feel.

Whether you choose to explore working with gemstones or crystals because they have a nice look and you enjoy their energetic effects or you wish to dig deeper into the magick contained in rock, make it personal to you. Explore working with stones with some of the suggested techniques in this chapter to see if you feel their power!

## Seeking Your Stone

Where do you even start when choosing a stone to begin a spirit ally partnership? In a similar fashion to how one begins a partnership with healing plant allies. There are several ways to go about starting a relationship with a stone. One option is to intuitively pick a stone and begin working with it. You might visit a crystal shop or look online and pick out a stone. Many crystal stores now offer live online sales or are willing to walk you around the store remotely to show you their selections. Once you have the particular stone you are drawn to, hold the stone and feel out its energies. How does the stone make you feel when you pick it up? What drew you to choose that particular stone? Was it its color, size, shape, or location? Do you feel like this stone is meant to partner with you for some objective? Your answers to these questions can sometimes help indicate the reason why you may be focusing on this partnership.

Another way to choose a stone to work with is by researching stones that are relevant to what you wish to work on. You might have a particular illness or symptom that you want assistance with, so it's totally viable to look it up and decide before purchasing the stone. In its own way, you're still choosing the stone to which you were most drawn. Once you have the stone, see how it feels when you hold it—some gemstones or crystals give off a vibration that can be felt. Oftentimes, I feel a kinship with the right stone for me once I've found it.

If you are doubting your intuitive abilities and not sure where to start with stones, you might choose a general stone like quartz crystal to begin a partnership. Quartz is an amplifying stone and can be beneficial to anything you are working on. It's a good stone to start with, as you may be able to sense its energy. Even if you can't, it likely will still partner well with you.

When you feel ready to create a relationship with the spirit of the stone you've chosen, you will ask the spirit of the stone to share a message with you. If you didn't research your stone when you picked it, meditate with the stone first and receive its message before you know its associations. The following is an exercise to help you do that.

## EXERCISE
### Communing with a Healing Stone Ally

Remember that although stone spirits can have specific meanings and areas of expertise, there may be an individual purpose, medicine, or energy specific to working with you. Do this exercise in a quiet, comfortable space. If you'd prefer, record the exercise and play back the instructions so you can follow along with the meditation. When you are finished, write down your experiences in a journal and keep track of how you perceive and connect with your healing stone ally.

#### You will need

Stone of your choosing
Incense such as frankincense or copal

#### Optional

A way to play soft music
A way to record and play back the meditation
A journal to record your experience

*Sit or lie down in a comfortable position, ensuring you're relaxed and at ease. Take a couple of deep breaths, inhaling and exhaling. Feel yourself grow roots that grow down deep to the core of Mother Earth. State your intention out loud: "I seek to commune with the spirit of my stone for my highest good at this time."*

*You are now entering into a meditative state where all you do is for your highest good. Envision the numbers as we count them down now. See the numbers twelve, eleven, ten, nine, eight, seven, six, five, four, three, two…*

*One. You find yourself in a cave made of stone. You see a smooth rock ahead of you that looks like a good place to rest. You feel comfortable and safe in this warm and earthy cavern. From your pocket or bag, you retrieve the stone that you wish to commune with. Holding the stone in your hand, you ask, "Do you have a message for me?" Be open to how the spirit presents itself. The spirit of the stone may appear as the stone itself, a personified being, or even a color of light. However it appears to you is most perfect for this exploration.*

*Ask the stone, "How may we work together for healing?" Be open to whatever answer is brought forward.*

*With gratitude, thank this stone ally for its healing, wisdom, and connection. You send a final blessing and receive any energy it may return to you. You stand and leave the cave knowing you can return whenever you choose. You bid thanks and farewell to the spirits of this place and to your healing stone ally.*

*Count up from your meditative state: one, two, three, four, five, six, seven, eight, nine, ten, eleven, twelve. Feel your fingers and toes gently stretching. When you are ready, you may open your eyes.*

Journal or write down the experiences, messages, or visions shared with you in this meditation. Know you can always repeat this exercise to commune with the spirit of your healing plant ally. Notice each time if your perception of it shifts or changes.

Some of my favorite ways of working with stone allies began with letting a stone call out to me. It could happen if I'm drawn to a crystal from a metaphysical store, a place in nature, or a sacred site. I love bringing home stones from sacred trips, even from spiritual conferences or retreats. Some stones I keep to create magickal jewelry using the stone or incorporating it into a charm or talisman.

## Stones for Chronic Illness and Healing

The following is a list of stones that are great for healing and living with chronic illness.

### *Angelite*

This stone is a powerful ally for connecting with your spirit guides, angels, and the celestial realm. It has a comforting energy, supports mediumship work, and keeps you feeling safe and supported. It aids in spirit communication by providing clarity for spirit messages. I found it quite interesting that angelite has an affinity for healing having to do with blood. It can also be helpful for throat issues and in the functioning of the heart. It also can provide rectification when sensory perceptiveness has been lost.

### *Black Tourmaline*

This is a protective stone used to prevent harm or negative energies. It provides mental and physical balance. It is an excellent stone to work with to protect yourself from any negative energies when working with the public, as well as from psychic attack. It promotes clear communication and enhances intuition. It can stimulate reflex points associated with the lower back. It is helpful for arthritis, dyslexia, heart disease, anxiety, and disorientation. It helps stimulate and balance the adrenal glands.

### *Bloodstone*

This green stone with red flecks is known as an intense healing stone and the stone of courage. It provides a strong grounding energy, and I've found it quite useful to help pull me back when I've been in a dysregulated state. Because its color changes, it is regarded as a shape-shifting stone that can aid those who walk between the worlds. It is also a powerful stone to work with while healing ancestral bloodlines or inherited illness. It is helpful in treatment of the spleen, to purify the blood, kidneys, bladder, intestines, and liver. It can neutralize toxins in the body. It also has an affinity for fixing eyesight, lung congestion, and rashes.

### *Chevron Amethyst*

This amethyst is an excellent problem-solving and healing stone. It has the inherent attributes of amethyst— it amplifies psychic awareness, intuition, and connection to the spirit world. It aids in opening the third eye, which enhances the ability to dream, meditate, strengthen divination, and banish unwanted habits and addictions. While having the amplified abilities of detecting and diagnosing health issues noted in one's auric field, it also assists in cleansing the aura. It can also help with inner-self evaluation and self-evolution. Chevron is said to help with disorders of the lungs, the intestines, the pancreas, and the liver. It can help to eliminate headaches, pain, and symptoms of viral and infectious diseases.

### *Chrysocolla*

This stone provides great inner strength and is said to offer endurance during stressful or long-standing situations. It helps boost physical vitality and aids with complicated grief. It can help purify your home and your surroundings because its energy is conducive to stabilizing the environment around where it is kept.

### *Citrine*

Citrine is a stone of creativity and empowerment. It can provide mental clarity and aid in decision-making. This stone has a soothing quality to it that provides optimism and comfort. Citrine promotes the circulation of blood, helps with degenerative disorders, is helpful for digestive disorders, facilitates the diminishment of growths, and balances thyroid issues.

### *Garnet*

A stone of health, garnet has the ability to extract negative energy from the body and transmute it to be beneficial. It discourages chaotic, disruptive, and disorganized growth and helps provide stabilization and order mentally, emotionally, psychically, and spiritually. It can aid disorders of the spine and spinal fluid, bone, cellular structure, heart, lungs, and blood. It helps absorb vitamins and process medications with fewer side effects. Garnet has regenerative forces and therefore assists in degenerative diseases.

### *Hematite*

Hematite is a stone of the mind. It helps with memory and mental clarity and assists in understanding knowledge. It is also an excellent stone to ground oneself. It is said to help promote courage, confidence, and emotional stability, and it makes for a helpful spirit ally if we need to adjust to the mundane world. Hematite helps the body cool off and is excellent for fevers. It has balancing properties and can help bring equilibrium to body systems. It is used to treat leg cramps, blood disorders like anemia, nervous system disorders, anxiety, and insomnia. It can also help align the spine and is a great choice to complement chiropractic treatments.

### *Jasper*

Jasper is a supreme nurturer stone. It offers protection and helps with grounding. It aids with balancing physical, emotional, and mental energies. It also is said to aid astral travel. Jasper can be used in the treatment of tissue deterioration of internal organs and disorders of the kidneys, spleen, bladder, liver, and stomach. It is helpful for COVID-19 symptoms and relieves loss of smell. It is also used to soothe nervousness and aids anxiety and PTSD.

### *Jet*

This fossil opens one to the connection and integration of ancient knowledge and ancestral wisdom. It can aid the grieving process and promote peaceful, calm energies. It dispels fearful thoughts and can protect against violence and illness. A great stone for depression, it also can be used in the treatment of migraine headaches, epilepsy, glandular and lymphatic swelling, stomach pain, and colds.

### *Kyanite*

Kyanite instantly aligns all chakras and subtle energy bodies, and it will not accumulate or retain negative energy or vibrations. It removes blockages and provides balance. It is a calming stone that brings peace and eases anxiety. It promotes clear communication and enhances intuition. It can be used in the treatment of disorders of the muscular and urogenital systems, adrenal glands, throat, parathyroid glands, and brain.

### *Lepidolite*

Lepidolite is excellent for stress reduction and depression. It is a stone of transition, helping you through tough situations and old patterns. It is a very helpful stone for the adjustment of receiving a new diagnosis. It can help with tendinitis, leg cramps, tight muscles and shoulders, and elimination. It helps stabilize blood flow and soothes the nervous system. It can be beneficial for people with all types of mental illness.

### *Malachite*

A stone of transformation, malachite helps adjust to changing situations and can provide insight into diagnoses. It has a balancing ability within the body. It encourages us to look deep within the self to acknowledge the reasons supporting an illness and can guide us to release emotional ties to our illness. It is said to protect against radiation and can be used in the treatment of asthma, arthritis, swollen joints, tumors, growths, broken bones, and torn muscles. It also enhances the immune system and can ease the process of giving birth.

### *Nuummite*

A protective and preventative stone, nuummite can shield on physical, mental, and emotional levels and also help prevent disease. It can enhance intellect and boost memory as well as aid intuition. Nuummite can be used in general healing and in tissue regeneration. It can help relieve pain and discomfort, especially headaches and degenerative disease. It helps disperse infections, purifies blood and the kidneys, and regulates insulin production. It has been used to treat disorders of the throat and the eyes. It's beneficial in strengthening eyesight as well as speech. It has an affinity for Parkinson's disease as well as disorders of the central nervous systems, disorders of the brain, and diabetes. It also aids anxiety and reduces stress.

### *Pearl*

Pearl is considered a stone of purity and brings truth to situations. It is helpful in accessing your higher truths as well as integrating wisdom. It has been used in the treatment of digestive disorders, to relieve bloat of bile issues, and to treat the body's soft organs. It also can increase fertility and ease childbirth.

### *Pyrite*

This stone helps keep away danger. It helps sustain health as well as intellect and emotional well-being. It also helps enhance memory. It can be used in the treatment of bones and matters of the lung, such as bronchitis. It has been used in the treatment of violent and/or highly infectious disease, as well as by others who are working with those affected to provide protection from the affliction. It can help lessen fevers and reduce inflammation.

### *Rose Quartz*

This pink quartz is a stone of compassion. It is connected with the heart center and can aid in keeping compassionate boundaries. It's an excellent stone to assist in delivering healing messages of love and creating an ambiance for healing. It can be used to aid in repairing cells in the body and to release impurities. It aids in clearing skin and the diminishment of disorders of the kidneys and adrenal glands. It can decrease coughs and issues of the lungs as well as relieve burns and blistering due to heat.

### *Selenite*

Selenite has a strong cleansing property. It provides clarity of the mind and expands awareness of the self and surroundings. It has been used to align the spinal column and also provides flexibility within the muscular structure. It has an affinity for skeletal system healing, as well as to stabilize epileptic disorders. It can be used to expand one's lifetime.

### *Tiger's Eye*

This is a stone of protection. It is excellent for grounding one's energy. It has a strong energy that helps one become calm and balanced. It helps provide focus and stimulates will, ambition, and discipline to those seeking spiritual development. It has been used to treat disorders of the eye, the throat, the reproductive system, and diverticular constrictions and to aid in night vision. It can also be used to strengthen the alignment of the spinal column and facilitate the mending of broken bones.

## Cleansing Stones

Before working with stones, it's important to cleanse them. Cleansing removes any energies, vibrations, or intentions that could be attached to the stone, returning it to its purest, most natural energetic state. Because stones can be cleansed, they can be repurposed and reprogrammed, so you don't need to buy another giant quartz tower after you've used it for that one spell or in the center of your crystal grid.

In addition to cleansing your crystals when you first receive them, it's good to clear their energy after prolonged use or intense work or after you've finished working with them for a specific purpose. This way, the crystal doesn't become foggy and full of the residual energies from those experiences. I have a stone table in my office where I conduct my readings, and I cleanse it each day so it doesn't absorb the energies from my sessions.

### EXERCISE
### Cleansing Stones in the Moonlight

Following is one cleansing method that I use.

#### You will need

A platter or a baking sheet to put stones on
An altar cloth or decorative cloth to put on the platter
The stones you wish to cleanse

**Step 1:** On the night before or on the full moon, place the altar cloth on the platter.

**Step 2:** Place the stones laid out on the platter.

**Step 3:** Place the stones outside in a spot where the moonlight can shine on the stones.

**Step 4:** Say aloud, *By the light of the moon, cleanse and clear these stones. So mote it be!*

**Step 5:** Leave the stones out in the moonlight.

**Step 6:** Before dawn, remove stones and bring them in the house. Do not let the daylight touch them.

### Alternative Methods

There are many ways to cleanse and clear stones.

- If they are not water-soluble stones, wash them in running water, such as a river.
- Place them in salt.
- Bury them in the ground for a moon cycle.
- Cleanse them with sacred smoke from burned herbs, sage, palo santo, or incense.

## Charging Stones

Stones can be charged with specific intentions. Programming crystals or stones offers a way to feel closer to the oversoul of that particular stone and work with it for a specific intention. You can charge stones for any purpose. I often work with the spirit of bloodstone. I find that it has an affinity for working with blood, which works out well for me because I have to monitor my blood on a regular basis to check my platelet levels.

To charge a stone, I might first seek out a piece of bloodstone that energetically and physically meets my needs. For example, I might choose a smooth stone I can hold in my hand that's small enough to be stored against my person. I often keep the stones I am working with in my bra for direct contact. If you don't wear a bra, keep the stone in your pocket, in a bag, on a necklace, or in a small satchel.

## EXERCISE
### Programming a Stone

Here's one good method for charging your healing stone.

#### You will need

The stone you wish to program
Power and Attraction Oil (recipe on page 80)

**Step 1:** Anoint the stone with an oil that is relevant to the work or use the Power and Attraction Oil.

**Step 2:** Tell the stone its specific purpose. You want to make sure you are programming the stone to focus on its abilities, which could be the attributes associated with the stone or what it has shared with you regarding your partnership. I use bloodstone as an example here, but tailor your words to your needs.

> *Bloodstone, green and red spirit ally of stone, I charge you to aid and assist in keeping my blood healthy and whole. Alert me to any changes or issues with my platelets or levels. Help me to be as healthy and well as possible. I thank you for this partnership and honor you. So mote it be.*

After programming, the stone will now directly work with its one intention until it is cleansed and reprogrammed.

## Heavy Energy Eaters

I learned another way to program a stone through my studies in the Temple of Witchcraft that has become a favorite. They suggest programming a stone as a "heavy energy eater."[16] I keep one of these in the room where I do my mediumship sessions and healing work. I also have one on my home altar. It also helps me with heavy emotions around illness, fear, grief, stress, worry, and anxiety. Any particular stone you feel called to work with can be used, though it is wise to choose one that has correspondences to protection and cleansing. I've used clear quartz, selenite, black river

16. Christopher Penczak, *The Temple of Shamanic Witchcraft: Shadows, Spirits, and the Healing Journey* (St. Paul, MN: Llewellyn Publishing, 2004), 143.

stones, and stones from my favorite lake. The purpose of the work is to ritually program the stone to be connected to the underworld, anchoring any heavy energy nearby that may arise. When heavy energy arises, it is transported via the stone and cord to the underworld to be transmuted; therefore, it doesn't hang around. It's a wonderful tool I have used at large festivals to eat any unwanted energy such as drama and chaos. For similar reasons, it is also great to bring with you if you need to stay in the hospital!

## Crystal Grids

A beneficial way to work with the healing power of crystals and stones is to make a crystal grid. Crystal grids are excellent for partnering with the spirits of stone and to amplify their focused intentions like promoting healing or reducing the impacts of symptoms or side effects of medications. Crystal grids are traditionally made by placing crystals in a grid formation, usually in patterns of sacred geometry. While there are specific clothes, boards, and designs that can be followed to create a pattern, once you get comfortable working with grids, they are easy to create with your own intuition and preferences. Anything you are already using your crystals for can be incorporated into a grid: it could be for healing, amplifying a particular intention or objective, or cleansing a space.

There are both simple techniques and more complicated systems. It's best to find what works for you through exploration and practice. Often my grids resemble wheels but you could also use healing symbols or other designs. Interspacing different crystals and other items that can transmit energy. While less traditional, I find power in crafting grids that include my stone, bone, and plant spirit allies, and I place fresh flowers or herbs, dried plant pressings, feathers, bones, teeth, shells, and other sacred items into my crystal grids. These can be beautiful energetic arrangements that produce powerful effects when activated. Explore what it feels like when only stones are present and then how the energy changes after incorporating other materials. Other patterns you can explore include spirals, hearts, symbols, or whatever designs come through when you partner with the spirits involved!

## EXERCISE
## Creating a Healing Crystal Grid

To create a simple crystal grid to amplify healing, find a comfortable, relaxed, and safe space for your grid that will not be disturbed. Pick out the crystals you wish to use in your healing crystal grid. If you aren't sure, quartz crystals are easy stones to work with, as they amplify energy and will help bring forth what you wish to manifest. To make a grid for your own personal space at home or in a hospital room, consider using chrysocolla, garnet, bloodstone, and lepidolite. Whatever you use, make sure it has been cleansed beforehand.

### You will need

Stones or other items you would like included in your crystal grid
A surface for your crystal grid
Paper and a pen

### Optional

Sacred smoke from incense, palo santo, or sacred herbs
Candles
Music to promote the energy you are working to achieve

**Step 1:** Cleanse the space using sacred smoke, candles, or music.

**Step 2:** Write out the intention for your crystal grid. Make the intention as clear as possible. You may even consider writing it as a petition. For example:

> *I ask the Goddess, God, and Great Spirit*
> *Under the watchful eyes of the ancestors*
> *To aid in my healing, alleviate my symptoms,*
> *And reduce the side effects from my medications.*
> *Help me understand and incorporate*
> *Messages brought forth about my health.*
> *For the highest, healing good, harming none,*
> *May the spirits of stone guide me.*

*Thank you for these blessings bestowed.*
*So mote it be.*

**Step 3:** Choose which crystals you would like to use in this grid. Use your intuition to guide your decisions. Use stones or other materials that resonate with your intention.

**Step 4:** Create a pattern for the grid. You can incorporate sacred geometry into your pattern or just create from the heart. Creating something that is aesthetically pleasing and has good energy flow is ideal.

**Step 5:** You may start from the inside or outside when laying out the crystals. If you have a significant stone ally that you would like to work with for this intention, place it in the center. Any stones from the list at the beginning of the exercise work well.

**Step 6:** When you are ready to activate your grid, get yourself into a relaxed state.

**Step 7:** State aloud the intention that you wrote in step 2, and place your written intention under the grid's center stone.

**Step 8:** Using a quartz point (if you have one) or your fingers, touch each stone to activate the grid for the intention you have set. You might even say "activate" aloud as you touch each point.

**Step 9:** State aloud your gratitude for the outcome: *I thank all the stone spirits for their aid in this healing crystal grid. So mote it be!*

You can leave your grid for however long you will be using this energy. If it is for a session or working, I might deactivate it after its completion. You can leave a grid up for a short amount of time or several days. Check in with the spirits of the stones and see if they have any suggestions for your work.

# CHAPTER 12
# Animal Spirits

Animal spirits offer another magickal partnership to aid us with traditional and unique challenges that chronically ill folx face. Humans are part of the animal kingdom, so working with animal energy may come more naturally to you if you find it challenging to connect with plant and stone allies. Connecting to and working with animal spirits offers us lessons and connections to wisdom and experiences we may be going through while sick or even dealing with other people.

Perhaps there has been an animal with which you've had an affinity your entire life. This may well be an animal spirit ally for you.

## Communing with a Healing Animal Ally

You can use meditation to ask for and be shown an animal spirit to work with for your chronic illness or specific needs. See what shows up and if it can be incorporated into your practice.

### EXERCISE
### Communing with a Healing Animal Ally

Do this exercise in a quiet, comfortable space. If you have the option, do this exercise out in nature where you might have the chance for a safe animal encounter. Record this exercise and play back the instructions so you can follow along with this meditation. When you are done, write down your experiences in a journal and keep track of how you perceive and connect with your animal allies.

### You will need

Incense such as frankincense or copal

### Optional

A way to play soft music
A way to record and playback the meditation
A journal to record your experience

*Sit or lie down in a comfortable position, ensuring you're relaxed and at ease. Take a couple of deep breaths, inhaling and exhaling. State your intention out loud: "I seek to commune with the spirits of the creatures of flesh and bone and meet with the most perfect healing animal ally for my highest good at this time."*

*You are now entering into a meditative state where all you do is for your highest good. Envision the numbers as we count them down now. See the numbers twelve, eleven, ten, nine, eight, seven, six, five, four, three, two…*

*One. See before you a crooked path leading into a sacred forest. As you enter the woods, you touch a guardian tree and announce yourself and your intentions for this special visit. Call from your heart and proclaim that you enter these woods as a friend, as a witch, or however you spiritually identify. You call out that you seek to commune with the spirits of the creatures of flesh and bone and meet a healing animal ally for your highest healing good. You walk forward along this path, and you feel your feet upon the cool earth and a light breeze on your skin. You sense the feeling of life around you. Notice the sound of these woods: the chirping of birds, the scurries of little creatures in the brush, the babbling of flowing water, trees creaking, whispering in the wind. You feel connected to this sacred land and all its spirits.*

*Ahead of you on this path, you see a thicket with a comfortable space for you to sit and commune with a healing animal ally. As you take a seat, you call to the healing animal ally that is just right for you at this time and seek its counsel.*

*Whatever shows up for you is most perfect for this experience. Commune with your healing animal ally and receive any wisdom or guidance it may share with you. Ask how you may partner with this animal in your healing practice. Is there healing offered to you from this animal? What is the wisdom and magick it shares with you?*

*With gratitude, thank this healing animal ally for its wisdom, healing, and connection. You send a final blessing and receive any energy that it may return to you. You stand and leave the grove and make your way back down the path until you leave the woods, knowing you can return whenever you choose. You bid thanks and farewell to the fauna and spirits of this place and to your animal ally.*

*Count up from your meditative state: one, two, three, four, five, six, seven, eight, nine, ten, eleven, twelve. Feel your fingers and toes gently stretching. When you are ready, you may open your eyes.*

Don't forget to journal or write down the experiences, messages, or visions shared with you in this meditation. You can always repeat this exercise to commune with the spirit of your healing animal ally. Notice each time if your perception of it shifts or changes.

## Animal Spirit Allies for Chronic Illness

Here's a list of some animal spirit allies who can help you with your chronic illness. This list is by no means exhaustive. It's possible for any animal to partner with you to help you understand what's showing up for you. They can provide wisdom and insight and, sometimes, the higher message in a situation. They can also empathize with what you are going through and be with you during the rough times. And they can be there to help pump you up too!

### *Badgers*

These hardcore, fierce creatures stand and hold their ground. They have claws they use to dig deep into the ground to get to the root of problems and healing. Badger can help us process our anger toward our illness and what shows up from it. Badger is one of the primary healing allies I work with and is a powerful ally if you are wanting to work on healing for all levels as well as continuing to fight the good fight in advocating for what you need.

### *Bats*

Bats are associated with liminal spaces. We see them come out at dusk, and they are able to navigate in the dark through sonar. Bats have connections to the cycles of life, death, and rebirth. They can be worked with for periods of transition and cycle endings. Bat can be a powerful ally when we are first diagnosed with a chronic illness and when our symptoms evolve or change. It can feel like a death and a rebirth when we go through this process, and Bat can help remind us that all is not lost; we are only becoming a new version of ourselves. Bat reminds us that we live in cycles and nothing is stagnant.

### *Bears*

The bear is a powerful ally for chronically ill folx. Bear hibernates and goes within to reflect on what has happened to them. If it is a stressful or confusing time, Bear encourages us to go in and find the answers inside of us while also being gentle with ourselves, reminding us that it can take time. Dream with Bear, and you may find some hidden wisdom that is most perfect for what you are seeking.

### *Beetles*

Beetles are associated with transformation and resurrection. They can help us in times of transition and transformation, often when it feels like our world is being torn down. Beetle can show up and remind us how we may build again. Call on Beetle to release and break down that which no longer works for you so transformation can occur.

### *Butterflies and Moths*

Often considered to be the spirits of evolution, butterflies are solar in nature and moths are lunar. Both have gone through their metamorphosis to transform into something beautiful and able to fly. Call to Butterfly and

Moth to aid you in your transformations, whether they are small steps or a big change.

### *Cats*

These creatures have a rich history associated with magick. They can sense spirits and are independent and cunning. Cat can be a helpful ally when you are craving independence. Ask Cat to guide you and lend you strength to make activities of daily living easier. You can also ask Cat for assistance when you work with doctor—specifically, knowing what is best to say and when.

### *Foxes*

Foxes are swift, cunning, and easily blend in with their environment. They have camouflage for all seasons. Call on Fox when you would like to blend in and go unnoticed, when you feel you need to be witty and articulate, or whenever you want to know how best to say what you want and when.

### *Goats*

The goat is sure-footed and able to navigate tricky terrains. Call on Goat when you feel like giving up or that the path you are on is too hard. Summon Goat's stubbornness to help press on and find your footing. Goats are also playful creatures, so Goat can also remind us that we have room in our life to push for what we want while also enjoying the stops along the way.

### *Horses*

Horses are fast and free. Horse's spirit is bold and charges bravely toward their destination, even if it is a great distance away. Work with Horse when you have a goal you wish to meet and are ready to move forward with force. Ride hard, and Horse will be there by your side.

### *Opossums*

These scavengers have the ability to feign their own death when they feel frightened or are in danger. Sometimes we need to allow ourselves to lie fallow for a bit and be a bit dead, so to speak. Allow yourself time to rest and recharge from whatever is frightening or threatening. When you are ready, resurrect yourself and keep plugging along!

### *Otters*

The otter shows up when we need some joy in our life. Has it been a serious time with heavy news or are you just feeling at your worst? If Otter is showing up, find whatever brings you some happiness and joy, and allow yourself to bask in it. Let go of worry and guilt just for now, and do what you can to be lifted up. I know how hard this can be in times of despair. So let Otter do some of the heavy lifting by calling on them to show you what you need.

### *Rabbits*

Rabbits have a long history associated with fear. If you find yourself spinning your wheels in dread or fear, call on Rabbit to help. Rabbit can lead the way and beckons you to follow down the rabbit hole to face your fears. Can you summon the courage needed to get through this time? Ask Rabbit for that help, and you'll be in good company.

### *Raccoons*

Raccoon is here to show us the masks we wear. What are we masking, and why? There may be valid reasons to not show the world our true colors for fear of repercussion. Maybe it is time to take off these masks and be our authentic selves and let those we fear accommodate us! Wherever you are with mask wearing, if Raccoon shows up, let them provide you with guidance and lessons on the masks being worn and how to move on with your best face forward!

### *Skunks*

These sweet creatures often get a bad reputation due to their powerful ability to spray. Because of this, they hold dominion over most of what they encounter. Skunk can teach us to embody self-confidence and use our power wisely, yet not be afraid to wield it. Call on Skunk when you need a mental health refresher on confidence boost... or when it's time to use the spray.

### *Snakes*

Snakes are associated with wisdom, transformation, initiation, and the mysteries of life and death. Snakes possess the ability to shed their skin, which we all need to do from time to time. Snake also connects us to our DNA and bloodlines. Call to Snake to seek the mysteries that flow through your blood and to bring healing and transmutation to your ancestral lines. This can be especially healing and beneficial if you know you have a hereditary condition or suspect your illness may have ancestral ties.

### *Wolves*

The wolf is a powerful pack animal used to being with others. If Wolf is showing up for you, assess where you are in relation to friends and family. Have you been distant as of late? It could be due to physical or mental health. Wolves take care of each other and can remind us to let ourselves be nurtured by those who love us if they are offering. Wolf can help us with acceptance of help or where we stand with family and friends, even if that is at a distance. Wolf can also help us search for our new pack when we are in transition or lonely.

## Pet Therapy

Having a pet can be one of the most rewarding and fulfilling things you can do with your life. When I have hosted Living a Magickal Life with Chronic Illness discussion groups, this topic never fails to come up. Oftentimes during the online video chat, a show-and-tell will naturally evolve as everyone's pets show up in their rooms. I notice everyone smiles and the energy shifts, alluding to the power and impact animals can have on people, especially folks with chronic illness.

Many of us with chronic illness end up spending a lot of time at home, whether we like it or not. Sharing space with an animal, caring for and feeding them, and especially spending quality time together can reap huge benefits. There are innumerable studies out there on why pet therapy programs are effective at reducing stress and lowering anxiety and depression. It has certainly been effective for me. I live on a farm with not only a menagerie of indoor creatures but an entire barn full. Spending time with the animals is one of my main sources of healing and regeneration.

I highly recommend seeking out an animal companion to live with. If that's not something you are able to do given your circumstances, find someone with a pet whom you can visit with to benefit from their energy. Pet therapy programs exist and are quite popular in nursing homes and health care settings. When I volunteered at hospices, I noticed that these programs were always the most requested and well received. Visiting animals at petting farms or rehab programs, volunteering to socialize animals at rescues, or finding other ways to be near the majestic presence of animals may well be worth the effort.

## The Healing Power of Animals

After I was discharged from the hospital from my initial blood disorder ordeal, I came home to a very new normal. I was not loving how I felt or how I was having to spend my days. I live on a farm, and there wasn't a lot I could do for those first few months. However, before I knew how sick I was, I bred my sweet pig Primrose. Shortly after I came home from the hospital, she had her babies. It was her first litter of piglets, but she did not take to motherhood. After attacking her babies, I had to pull the remaining living piglets away from her so she wouldn't kill them. I ended up with nine little squealing babies that I was going to have to feed and care for until they were old enough to survive on their own. I set up my downstairs bathroom as piglet central and worked hard to feed everyone. With the help of my veterinarian's office, all the piglets survived that crucial first week of life. Taking care of these piglets took a lot of work, but I rose to the occasion. I had been sick and depressed before I had the newfound goal of caring for these piglets. My favorite out of all the pigs was the runt, Teenyweeny.

Teenyweeny quickly bonded with me and became my close companion. She slept in my room next to my bed in her own heated piglet house, and often she slept in bed with me. I loved that piglet so wholeheartedly,

I started to live for her. She gave me a reason to live in those first very dark days. And though this story ends in a tragic way, I spent eight significant weeks doing everything in my power to keep her alive, and in return, she did the same for me. When she had to be euthanized due to a severe neurological issue, I was devastated but knew we had the time together for a very real reason. I'll be forever grateful to her for that.

## EXERCISE
### Spend Time with an Animal

Spending time with animals is a great way to help yourself feel better. Petting animals is known to reduce feelings of loneliness or isolation, encourage communication, and provide comfort during stressful times. Additionally, it can decrease depression and anxiety levels.

#### You will need

Access to a friendly dog, cat, or other animal

Pat, play, or just be around this animal. Notice if your mood changes. How do you feel? Better than before? I bet so!

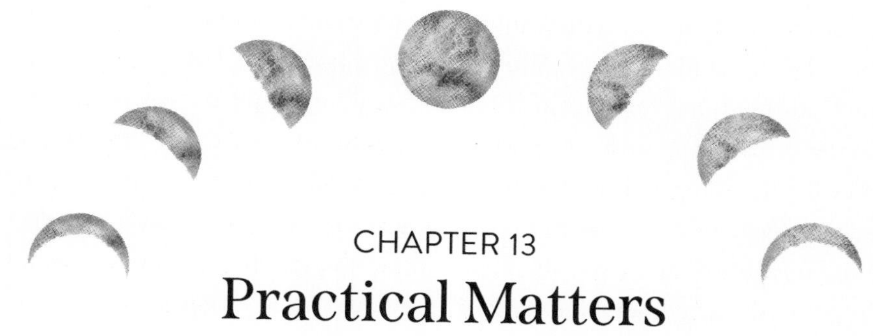

CHAPTER 13

# Practical Matters

As we near the end of our journey together, I hope that in this last section I can provide some guidance around practical matters of living with chronic illness. These topics walk hand in hand with our magickal work and will make the world a better place for folks experiencing health challenges.

## Confronting Our Mortality

If you have read my previous work or have ever attended a Death Cafe or one of the Mortal Musing discussion groups I facilitate, then you likely know how passionate I am about "good death." Having a good death starts with talking about death. We're all going to die—that's the only certainty in life. Some of us may have conditions that could mean we have a shorter life than others. Some of us have no idea how our chronic illnesses and health challenges will play out longevity-wise. We do know that thinking and talking about death and your end-of-life plans will not kill you, contrary to what you may feel.

I encourage you and everyone you know to talk about how you ideally and in the best-case scenario would like your death plan to go. This includes filling out advance directives and a living will. Advance directives are any legal forms that guide your future medical care. One type of advance directive that is crucial to have in place is a living will. A living will is a specific document that shapes end-of-life treatment. Living wills allow you to state what you would and would not like to happen to you in the case you could not speak for yourself. Who would you want to make medical decisions for you in this case? How extreme do you want life-saving measures to be taken, and how long should your care team prolong your life if, for example, you were in a vegetative state? There is lots to consider, and there are no right or wrong answers. My partner wants everything possible done to save them, including keeping them on life support. I do not wish to be hooked up to machines and would rather have someone make the tough decisions on my behalf so I can be at peace.

Once you designate someone as your health care proxy—the decision-maker for your health care choices—make sure you tell them *and* they are on board with this responsibility. Without that crucial conversation, you might blindside someone, and it could result in a difficult scenario for all involved. Discuss your feelings and opinions at length on how you would handle medical situations. And of course, don't be afraid to change your mind as time passes. For now, I want to try to be saved and have resuscitation efforts done on me, but if I was very frail and not doing well and the process could break my ribs and make things plausibly unlivable, I may opt for a DNR (Do Not Resuscitate) order. I used to want my sister to make decisions for me, especially around end of life situations. However, now that I've spent lots of time in hospitals and going through a life-threatening episode, I know my partner can handle it. We've spent lots of time together going over my feelings and wants as well as my absolute nos.

It's also important to think on and convey how you want your funeral care to be. What kind of body disposition do you want—cremation, burial, or something else? Do you want a traditional type of funeral? Do you want a wake? Do you want to be embalmed? If you are cremated, where or to whom do you want your remains to go to? These are just some prompts to get your mind turning. It doesn't have to be a gloomy thing.

Having a death plan is an incredible gift for your family and friends who will be making arrangements for you. Even if this subject challenges you, I encourage you to move through it at your own pace. Having your loved ones communicate their wishes to you, especially if you will be making decisions, also avoids the heavy burden of trying to guess what they want, never knowing if you did what they would have done. It is ultimately best to have these conversations before you are in crisis. Do this when everyone is well and able to before a time comes when you'll wish you had.

Thinking about death and talking about death can make us appreciate our own lives and what we wish to accomplish in our finite time here. It has helped me, and I hope it helps not only you but all your loved ones around you too.

## Resurrecting Self

One of the hardest things I've encountered is feeling so incredibly sick because of my health episode or chronic state that I just don't have the will or energy to do anything. What can you do? First, I think it is completely normal to feel upset and overwhelmed over the predicament. Often the best thing we can do is honor whatever feelings are showing up. If you're depressed or sad, that is okay. If you feel optimistic and like a warrior, excellent. It's unlikely you will consistently stay in one state. One thing I've tried before is "resurrecting" myself from the hole I was in during a stretch of bad times. This practice does take a certain amount of emotional, mental, and spiritual energy, so I recognize it may not work for all the bad times. It's okay to just be in it and not focus on anything else besides getting through the rough stuff.

To do the resurrection spell, you must find within yourself the will to push through what is happening to you. When you feel it can be summoned, speak freely from your heart as to why you wish to be resurrected. Here I've crafted a simple incantation that may be used in conjunction with your own heartfelt call.

*In the darkest hours of the darkest days,*
*I reach into myself to find my own way,*
*That will empower and awaken what lies within me,*
*So I may be more myself with a turn of the key,*

*Alive and healing, I am moving toward whole;*
*I resurrect myself—mind, body, and soul.*

I've found the outcome of this spell for myself has to do with acceptance or getting to a place of acceptance, but this alone can be a huge shifting point. Acceptance of what is terrible and true at the moment while knowing this is not a permanent state is powerful. Things will change and you won't be in whatever state you are in right now forever. Resurrecting your best self can pull you from the depths of despair, allowing you to face the challenges and move through it.

## The Wounded Healer

There have been times I've been challenged by the comment "If you are such a good witch, why can't you heal yourself?" If anyone has every confronted you to say this and it left you feeling incapable or questioning yourself, I encourage you to meditate on the archetypal Wounded Healer or perhaps Chiron, the wounded healer in Greek mythology. Chiron was wounded accidentally by Heracles's poisonous arrow, said to be coated with the toxic blood of the Hydra. An immortal centaur, Chiron could not die from the wound, so it continued to be a painful burden to him. However, Chiron was a gifted healer and continued to offer his services to the world, healing the sick and injured.

Swiss psychologist Carl Jung coined the archetypal term "wounded healer," and it refers to people who have gone through painful experiences or trauma that enables them to help and heal others. Wounded healers are better able to empathize, accept, and listen to others about what they've been through. Oftentimes, wounded healers end up in helping professions and, like Chiron, offer their aid even if they still have trauma, mental health challenges, ongoing pain, or illness they are going through. These people are often well-versed, knowledgeable, and willing to share information or potentially helpful resources with others.

## Toning the Vagus Nerve

One technique that has helped me with my mental health as it relates to how I feel physically is resetting or "toning" the vagus nerve. *Vagus* in Latin means "wandering," and the vagus nerve is likewise not one nerve but thousands of fibers organized into two bundles that run down the brain stem through each side of the neck, into the torso, and branch (or wander) outward to touch all internal organs. It is often likened to a tree, where the branches interact with nearly all the body's organ systems. The vagus nerve picks up information about how the organs are functioning and also sends information from the brain stem back to the body, helping to control digestion, heart rate, voice, mood, and the immune system. The vagus is the main nerve of the parasympathetic nervous system. Unlike the sympathetic nervous system, which is associated with the body's "fight or flight" response, the parasympathetic branch helps us rest, digest, and calm down.[17]

Studies suggest that stimulating the vagus nerve can help in treatments for epilepsy, diabetes, treatment-resistant depression and post-traumatic stress disorder, as well as inflammatory arthritis conditions such as Crohn's disease and rheumatoid arthritis. There is also some interesting preliminary research that suggests that long COVID symptoms could originate, in part, from the virus's effect on the vagus nerve.

Here are a few methods to help you tone or reset your vagus nerve. Try these exercises and see what results you get. I can feel the difference, and I hope they are as helpful for you as they are for me.

### EXERCISE
### Cold Water Method

One of the ways you can tone the vagus nerve is to hold your breath and submerge your face in cold water. This can trigger what's known as the diving reflex, which is a response that slows the heartbeat and constricts blood vessels. Some people who have tried it report that it has a calming effect and can even reduce insomnia. Others wrap an ice pack in cloth and

17. Christina Caron, "This Nerve Influences Nearly Every Internal Organ. Can It Improve Our Mental State, Too?" *New York Times*, accessed January 22, 2024, https://www.nytimes.com/2022/06/02/well/mind/vagus-nerve-mental-health.html.

place it on their chest to relieve anxiety. I have done this with success and think it's worth trying if you are in a heightened state of anxiety.

### You will need

Access to a sink and cold water
Ice cubes
Towel

**Step 1:** Fill a sink with cold water. Add in some ice cubes to get the water to a cold temperature.

**Step 2:** Notice how you feel at the start of this exercise. It is good to do when you are in a heightened state of anxiety, but it's just as useful whenever you believe you need it.

**Step 4:** Make sure the hair is out of your face and your glasses are off. When you are ready, take a deep breath and submerge your head into the cold water. Keep your head submerged as long as you can.

**Step 5:** When you cannot hold your breath any longer, take your head out of the sink.

**Step 6:** Notice how you are feeling. Can you feel a difference from before?

**Step 7:** Towel dry your face and drain the sink.

## EXERCISE
## Slow Belly Breathing Method

Another way to stimulate and tone the vagus nerve is through deep, slow belly breathing. Working with breathing exercises to shift the focus from stress or pain can be beneficial for a multitude of reasons; this is one. Rhythmic breathing in which you breathe more slowly (optimally aiming for six breaths per minute) will stimulate the vagus nerve. Breathing more deeply from the belly while expanding your abdomen and widening your rib cage as you inhale is great. Exhale longer than it takes for you to inhale to trigger a relaxation response.

## EXERCISE
### Vagus Nerve Neck Exercise

Guided by a therapist, I have tried numerous ways to stimulate my vagus nerve. Try this neck exercise, and see how you feel—it's one of the easiest and most popular ways.

**Step 1:** Lie on your back.

**Step 2:** Interweave fingers on both hands and place behind head.

**Step 3:** Without turning your head, look to the right.

**Step 4:** Remain here until you spontaneously yawn or swallow.

**Step 5:** Return to a neutral position with head and eyes straight.

**Step 6:** Repeat on the other side.

## EXERCISE
### The Half Salamander

Another method to try is called the Half Salamander:

**Step 1:** Look right without turning your head.

**Step 2:** Tilt your head to the right, toward your shoulder.

**Step 3:** Hold for thirty to sixty seconds.

**Step 4:** Then return eyes and head straight back to a neutral position.

**Step 5:** Look left without turning your head.

**Step 6:** Tilt your head to the left, toward your shoulder.

**Step 7:** Hold for thirty to sixty seconds.

**Step 8:** Return to a neutral position.

### Half-Salamander Variation

One variation is to look in the opposite direction of the head tilt: when the head tilts left, the eyes look right and vice versa. As before, hold your neck for thirty to sixty seconds.

## Considerations for Communities

As I've connected with folks about community participation at public ritual events, I've heard some horror stories. As a result, I now reflect and talk more with folks about making events or group activities more accessible for all, including those with chronic illness and beyond. A lot of these considerations are basic and would be easy to implement. Some require a little more planning but can absolutely be done for everyone to have a better experience. The key here is speaking up and asking for what you need. In a better world, we wouldn't have to do this, but accessibility is the norm. Do your best to speak up about needs at the spaces you frequent.

### *Access and Accommodations*

One suggestion for accommodation is to make sure chairs are available for folks to sit in. If people are unable to stand during ritual, chairs allow them to be comfortable and still participate. If it's a larger ritual, reserve seating for disability access and for those with hearing or seeing impairments. Tying up hair and wearing lipstick can be of assistance to those who lip-read. Having a deaf interpreter at events is also a great way to ensure all can participate. Having printed materials is also helpful for comprehension and access. Avoiding incense or scents for rituals can make a world of difference for those who are sensitive to smell. If you are running an event, make sure that signs are clearly marked or that volunteers are able to direct those in need of handicap accessibility to restrooms, elevators, water stations, and exits.[18]

18. Amy Blackthorn, *Blackthorn's Botanical Wellness: A Green Witch's Guide to Self-Care* (Newburyport, MA: Weiser Books, 2022).

### *Finding a Cofacilitator*

Something I've run into several times over the past few years as I've been living with being too sick to do things more often is when it conflicts with teaching/presenting/running an event. When you have chronic illness, sometimes you need to cancel. You have no choice. If you are running something, canceling can be a big problem. What has saved my butt on numerous occasions is having a cofacilitator when possible. I cofacilitate Mortal Musings, an online discussion group held regularly through the Temple of Witchcraft, and I've just started a Living a Magickal Life with Chronic Illness discussion group. These both have multiple people leading so when I have had to bail on Mortal Musings, the event could still be held. It's something I try to avoid doing, but you never know what each day will hold when you are having ongoing health issues.

### *Providing Online Options*

Having online options for classes and rituals can make a world of difference for someone who has a hard time going out for myriad reasons. I hope to see more hybrid in-person and online classes and rituals in the future. My community has been doing two separate rituals, which is also a kind and smart idea.

### *Be Honest*

I'm a psychic medium and see clients remotely these days but occasionally, I will need to reschedule folks because I am sick. When I was hospitalized and in the year that followed, I spent so much angst on having to cancel or move folks, sometimes multiple times. It ate me up how awful it felt to do it. I found myself flailing a bit and even discounting my services because I needed to move a session. Now, I include up front that I have a chronic illness and it is possible that I will need to move a session. If clients agree to that possibility, they can book with me. It has given my mind a lot of peace knowing that people understand from the beginning.

Another accommodation I made for myself after being diagnosed was keeping a schedule that suited my needs. I no longer read for folks at night and avoid doing evening events as much as possible. I know I am fried at the end of the day and function better early on, so that's what I now plan for. It's working out splendidly!

## Living the Best Life You Can

Even with chronic illness, you still have so much life to live, though it may look different from what you expected or is not quite what you envisioned. Yet the truth remains: you are a powerful witch weaving magick into the world. You can enchant your life. So much has yet to be accomplished, and you might not even realize the full potential of what could be. Your perspective is outside the normal, and you may feel like an outsider too. That is the path of the witch. There is power in being an outsider, and finding "the others" like yourself can be empowering. Meet other chronically ill witches. Join a group like the Temple of Witchcraft's Living a Magickal Life with Chronic Illness discussion group. Create your own space for community or evolve one out of your existing communities. Don't be afraid to take up space, for the community is greater for your involvement. Your contributions matter. And my feeling based on my experiences is that the more you allow yourself to be part of a community, the stronger you become on your own.

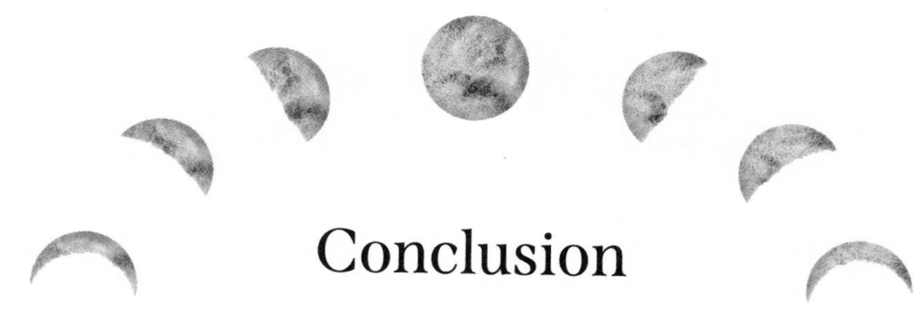

# Conclusion

I hope this book has given you comfort as well as some ideas on how to navigate witchcraft as well as the mundane world while being chronically ill. While there is no panacea, no cure-all to offer you, these techniques and ideas have helped me significantly as I've made my way through. Finding easier hacks to save yourself time and energy so you can use your will elsewhere is one way to add some power and control back into your life.

Reminding yourself that you can still be effective at magic and participate in witchcraft is a step toward gaining your power. You are not alone, this is not your fault, and you are still a powerful witch capable of great things. Facing a health crisis is scary, disappointing, frustrating, and downright difficult. Finding yourself on a journey to healing and living better days can be equally all those things. It is an initiation. It changes you on a deeper level and can never be undone.

There is no returning to the past; there is only going through and to the other side. The path is an ordeal, and it comes with its own ceremonies and rites. Titles may be bestowed upon you, and you may enter a community with others facing similar circumstances. To those acquainted with witchcraft traditions or ceremonial orders, these rituals may seem familiar. I welcome you to the Chronically Magickal tradition. Please remember your worth and that the contributions you offer to your communities and traditions matter.

# Recommended Reading


Auryn, Mat. *Mastering Magick: A Course in Spellcasting for the Psychic Witch*. Woodbury, MN: Llewellyn Publications, 2022.

Auryn, Mat. *Psychic Witch: A Metaphysical Guide to Meditation, Magick & Manifestation*. Woodbury, MN: Llewellyn Publications, 2020.

Blackthorn, Amy. *Blackthorn's Botanical Wellness: A Green Witch's Guide to Self-Care*. Newburyport, MA: Weiser Books, 2022.

Davis, K. C. *How to Keep House While Drowning: A Gentle Approach to Cleaning and Organizing*. New York: Simon and Schuster, 2020.

Dionne, Danielle. *Magickal Mediumship: Partnering with the Ancestors for Healing and Spiritual Development*. Woodbury, MN: Llewellyn Publications, 2020.

Fennell, Patricia A. *The Chronic Illness Workbook: Strategies and Solutions for Taking Back Your Life*. Oakland, CA: New Harbinger Publications, 2001.

Murphy-Hiscock, Arin. *The Witch's Book of Self-Care: Magical Ways to Pamper, Soothe, and Care for Your Body and Spirit*. Avon, MA: Adams Media, 2018.

Palmer, Amanda. *The Art of Asking: How I Learned to Stop Worrying and Let People Help*. New York: Grand Central Publishing, 2014.

Penczak, Christopher. *The Casting of Spells: Creating a Magickal Life through the Words of True Will.* Salem, NH: Copper Cauldron Publishing, 2016.

Penczak, Christopher. *The Inner Temple of Witchcraft: Magick, Meditation, and Psychic Development.* St. Paul, MN: Llewellyn Publications, 2002.

Penczak, Christopher. *The Outer Temple of Witchcraft: Circles, Spells, and Rituals.* St. Paul, MN: Llewellyn Publications, 2008.

Penczak, Christopher. *The Temple of Shamanic Witchcraft: Shadows, Spirits, and the Healing Journey.* St. Paul, MN: Llewellyn Publications, 2004.

Taylor, Sonya Renee. *The Body Is Not an Apology, Second Edition: The Power of Radical Self-Love.* Oakland, CA: Berrett-Koehler Publishers, 2018.

Ward, Terence P. *Empty Cauldrons: Navigating Depression through Magic and Ritual.* Woodbury, MN: Llewellyn Publications, 2022.

Wigington, Patti. *Witchcraft for Healing: Radical Self-Care for Your Mind, Body, and Spirit.* Emeryville, CA: Rockridge Press, 2020.

Zakroff, Laura Tempest. *Anatomy of a Witch: A Map to the Magical Body.* Woodbury, MN: Llewellyn Publications, 2021.

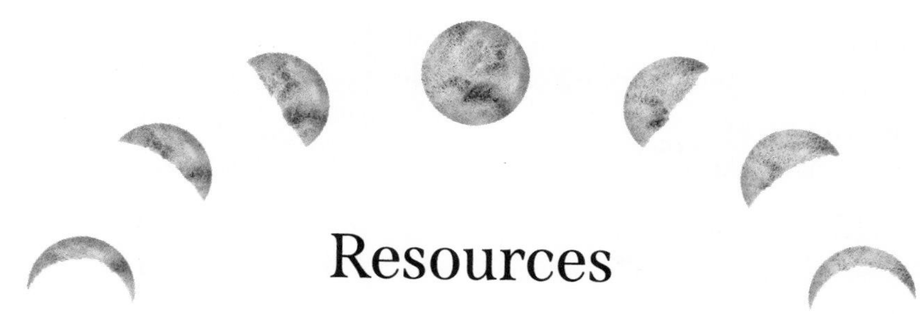

# Resources

**988 Suicide & Crisis Lifeline:** Call or text 988 for 24-7, free support for people in distress. Also provides prevention and crisis resources for you or your loved ones and best practices for professionals. (Chat option is also available at 988lifeline.org.)

**Veterans Crisis Line:** Veterans and their loved ones can call 988 and press 1, chat online, or send a text message to 838255 to receive confidential support 24 hours a day, 7 days a week, 365 days a year. Support for deaf and hard of hearing individuals is available.

**Crisis Text Line:** Free, 24-7 support for those in crisis. Text 741741 from anywhere in the US to text with a trained Crisis Counselor.

**The National Maternal Mental Health Hotline:** Provides free 24-7 confidential support, resources, and referrals to pregnant and postpartum mothers (and their loved ones) facing mental health challenges. Call or text 1-833-TLC-MAMA (1-833-852-6262).

**Trans Lifeline:** Call 1-877-565-8860 for a hotline staffed by transgender people for transgender people. Trans Lifeline volunteers are ready to respond to whatever support needs community members might have.

**Disaster Distress Helpline:** Call 1-800-985-5990 for a 24-7 national hotline dedicated to providing immediate crisis counseling for people who are experiencing emotional distress related to any natural or human-caused disaster.

**The Trevor Project:** A national 24-hour, toll free confidential suicide hotline for LGBTQ youth. If you are a young person in crisis, feeling suicidal, or are in need of a safe and judgment-free place to talk, call 1-866-488-7386 to connect with a trained counselor.

**The LGBT National Help Center:** 1-888-843-4564. Open to callers of all ages. Provides peer-counseling, information, and local resources.

## Resources for Finding a Therapist

*Psychology Today*
https://www.psychologytoday.com/

*American Psychological Association's Psychologist Locator*
https://locator.apa.org/

*National Register of Health Services Psychologists*
https://www.findapsychologist.org/

# Bibliography

Auryn, Mat. *Psychic Witch: A Metaphysical Guide to Meditation, Magick & Manifestation*. Woodbury, MN: Llewellyn Publications, 2020.

Blackthorn, Amy. *Blackthorn's Botanical Wellness: A Green Witch's Guide to Self-Care*. Newburyport, MA: Weiser Books, 2022.

Fennell, Patricia A. *The Chronic Illness Workbook: Strategies and Solutions for Taking Back Your Life Strategies and Solutions for Taking Back Your Life*. Oakland, CA: New Harbinger Publications, 2001.

Foor, Daniel. *Ancestral Medicine*. Rochester, VT: Bear & Company, 2017.

Hunter, Devin. *The Witch's Book of Power*. Woodbury, MN: Llewellyn Publications, 2016.

Jacqueline, Ilana. *Surviving and Thriving with an Invisible Chronic Illness: How to Stay Sane and Live One Step Ahead of Your Symptoms How to Stay Sane and Live One Step Ahead of Your Symptoms*. Oakland, CA: New Harbinger Publications, 2018.

Kübler-Ross, Elizabeth. *On Death and Dying*. New York: The Macmillan Company, 1969.

Murphy-Hiscock, Arin. *The Witch's Book of Self-Care: Magical Ways to Pamper, Soothe, and Care for Your Body and Spirit*. Avon, MA: Adams Media, 2018.

Palmer, Amanada. *The Art of Asking: How I Learned to Stop Worrying and Let People Help*. New York: Grand Central Publishing, 2014.

Penczak, Christopher. *The Casting of Spells: Creating a Magickal Life Through the Words of True Will*. Salem, NH: Copper Cauldron Publishing. 2016.

———. *The Outer Temple of Witchcraft: Circles, Spells, and Rituals*. Woodbury, MN: Llewellyn Publications, 2008.

———. *The Temple of Shamanic Witchcraft: Shadows, Spirits, and the Healing Journey*. St. Paul, MN: Llewellyn Publications, 2004.

Rosenberg, Stanley. *Accessing the Healing Power of the Vagus Nerve: Self-Help Exercises for Anxiety, Depression, Trauma, and Autism*. Berkeley, CA: North Atlantic Publishing, 2017.

Taylor, Sonya Renee. *The Body Is Not an Apology, Second Edition: The Power of Radical Self-Love*. Oakland, CA: Berrett-Koehler Publishers, 2018.

Wigington, Patti. *Witchcraft for Healing: Radical Self-Care for Your Mind, Body, and Spirit*. Emeryville, CA: Rockridge Press, 2020.

yronwode, catherine. *Hoodoo Herb and Root Magic: A Materia Magica of African-American Conjure*. Forestville, CA: Lucky Mojo Curio Company, 2002.

Zakroff, Laura Tempest. *Anatomy of a Witch: A Map to the Magical Body A Map to the Magical*. Woodbury, MN: Llewellyn Publications, 2021.

## Online Sources

Caron, Christina. "This Nerve Influences Nearly Every Internal Organ. Can It Improve Our Mental State, Too?" *New York Times* website. June 2, 2022. https://www.nytimes.com/2022/06/02/well/mind/vagus-nerve-mental-health.html.

Cherry, Kendra. "Spiritual Bypassing as a Defense Mechanism" Very Well Mind website. Updated March 17, 2023. https://www.verywellmind.com/what-is-spiritual-bypassing-5081640.

Color Psychology website. Accessed August 1, 2023. https://www.colorpsychology.org/.

"History and Traditions of Reiki." International Association of Reiki Practitioners website. accessed July 23, 2023 from https://iarp.org/history-of-reiki.

"How to Overcome Self-Limiting Beliefs." *Integrity Coaching and Leadership Development* (blog). Accessed August 18, 2023. https://www.integritycoaching.co.uk/blog/overcoming-the-challenges-of-headship/self-limiting-beliefs.

Laurie, Erynn Rowan. "The Cauldron of Poesy Text." Seanet website. Accessed January 16, 2024. https://www.seanet.com/~inisglas/cauldronpoesy.html#poesytext.

Lipman, Natasha. "Q&A: Pacing & Chronic lllness." Natasha Lipman website. January 20, 2020. https://natashalipman.com/qa-pacing-chronic-lllness-resting-pain-fatigue.

Miserandino, Christine. "The Spoon Theory." But You Don't Look Sick website. Accessed January 18, 2024. https://butyoudontlooksick.com/articles/written-by-christine/the-spoon-theory.

Misty Meadows Herbal Apprenticeship Program website. Accessed March 20, 2022. www.MistyMeadows.org.

Mountain Rose Herbs. "Guide to Tea Blending." Accessed March 23, 2022. https://blog.mountainroseherbs.com/guide-tea-blending.

Perry, Elizabeth. "The benefits of shadow work and how to use it in your journey." BetterUp website, June 13, 2022. https://www.betterup.com/blog/shadow-work.

Picciotto, Gabriela, Jesse Fox, Félix Neto. "A phenomenology of spiritual bypass: Causes, consequences, and implications." *Journal of Spirituality in Mental Health* 20, no. 4 (2018): 333–354. doi:10.1080/19349637.2017.1417756.

Moon, Tom. "The Four Liberating Questions." The Work of Byron Katie website. Accessed Sept 15, 2023. https://thework.com/2017/10/four-liberating-questions.

Raab, Diana. "Are You a Wounded Healer?" *The Empowerment Diary* (blog) via Psychology.com website. Accessed September 5, 2023.

https://www.psychologytoday.com/us/blog/the-empowerment-diary/202201/are-you-wounded-healer.

"Real Monsters." Zesty Does Things website. Accessed August 20, 2023. https://www.zestydoesthings.com/realmonsters.

Thomas, Halle M. "5 Tips for Chronic Illness Burnout from a Chronic Illness Therapist." *Chicory Counseling* (blog). Accessed September 20, 2023. https://www.chicorycounseling.com/blog/5-tips-for-chronic-illness-burnout-from-a-chronic-illness-therapist.

Tonkin, Lois. "Growing Around Grief." Cruse Bereavement Support website. Accessed July 29, 2023. https://www.cruse.org.uk/understanding-grief/effects-of-grief/growing-around-grief.

"What Is Integrated Energy Therapy® (IET®)?" LearnIET website. Accessed January 22, 2024. https://www.learniet.com.

## To Write to the Author

If you wish to contact the author or would like more information about this book, please write to the author in care of Llewellyn Worldwide Ltd. and we will forward your request. Both the author and publisher appreciate hearing from you and learning of your enjoyment of this book and how it has helped you. Llewellyn Worldwide Ltd. cannot guarantee that every letter written to the author can be answered, but all will be forwarded. Please write to:

Danielle Dionne
℅ Llewellyn Worldwide
2143 Wooddale Drive
Woodbury, MN 55125-2989

Please enclose a self-addressed stamped envelope for reply, or $1.00 to cover costs. If outside the U.S.A., enclose an international postal reply coupon.

Many of Llewellyn's authors have websites with additional information and resources. For more information, please visit our website at http://www.llewellyn.com.

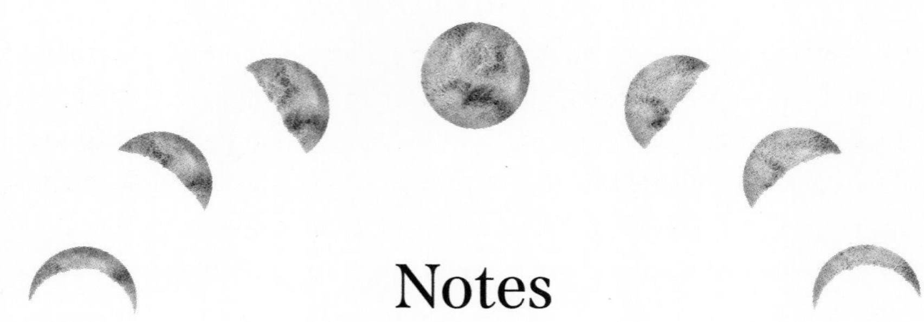

# Notes

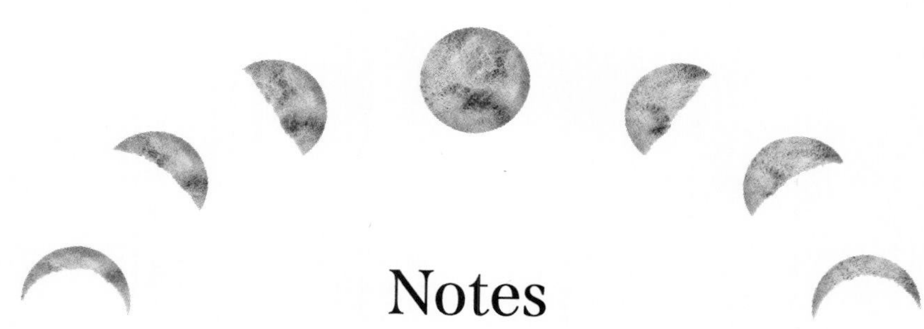

# Notes

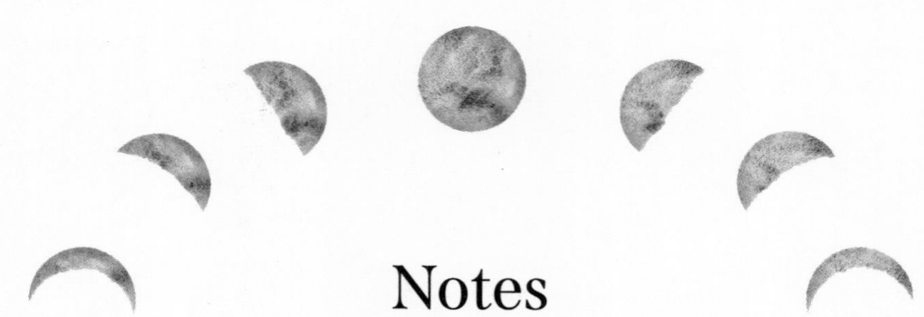

# Notes